FREE
TO FEE

How To Move Into The World Of Professional Speaking

Dr. Michael Soon Lee, CSP

Bill Cole MS MA

ABP

Special discounts on bulk quantities of Albert-Brownson Publishing books are available to corporations, professional associations, govern-mental entities and other organizations to use as sales promotions, premiums and training resources. Private imprints may also be arranged. For details, contact Albert-Brownson Publishing, 19925 Stevens Creek Blvd., Suite 100, Cupertino, CA 95014-2358, 408-725-7191.

International rights and foreign translations available only through negotiation with Albert-Brownson Publishing.

Library of Congress Cataloging In Publication Data

Soon Lee, Michael, and Cole, William B. Free To Fee: How To Move Into The World Of Professional Speaking

1. Reference 2. Communication 3. Business I. Title
ISBN: 978-1-931825-15-3: $19.95

TABLE OF CONTENTS

Award-Winning Professional Speakers Share Their Strategies For Going From Free To Fee

Working With Meeting Planners And Attendees

Resources For Professional Development

Business Resources For Speaking

About The Authors

Disclaimer

This book was written to provide information on speaking topics, platform skills, sales and marketing, fee setting, product development and career-building strategies about the world of professional speaking.

The authors and publisher are not engaged in rendering legal, accounting, psychological, career, counseling or other professional advice or services. If assistance of this type is sought, the services of the appropriate, competent professional should be consulted.

This publication does not contain all the available information about professional speaking available to potential or current speakers. It instead attempts to supplement, support and add to existing texts and other information sources. The reader is encouraged to consult all pertinent available material, in all published forms, and adapt and customize the material to your specific speaking needs.

Professional speaking is not a get-rich-quick business. This book does not purport or suggest that the professional speaking business is easy to enter, easy to make money in, nor easy to stay in. Professional speaking is a challenging industry, one that has risks, as any other business has. Anyone attempting to enter this field should expect to invest considerable time, money and effort to reach a level of success. Many individuals have transitioned to professional speaking and have made solid, profitable careers that have lasted for years.

The authors and publisher have made every effort to make this text as accurate and complete as possible. There may be, however, mistakes, both typographical and in content. Accordingly, this book should be used only as a general guide and not as the ultimate authoritative source on the speaking industry. This publication contains information on the speaking business that is current only up to the printing date.

The purpose of this text is to educate and to entertain. The authors and the publisher, Albert-Brownson Publishing, shall have neither liability nor responsibility to any person or entity with respect to any loss or damage caused or alleged to have been caused, directly or indirectly, by the information contained in this book.

If you do wish to be bound by the above, you may return this book to the publisher for a full refund.

Acknowledgements

We would like to acknowledge the important people who helped us in the writing and production of this book.

We would also like to thank those people who helped us in our speaking careers, either directly, or indirectly.

We would like to specifically thank members of the National Speakers Association (NSA), where we met an amazing collection of high-achieving individuals. We were very grateful to be a part of that organization and to have found a number of new speaking colleagues and friends there.

We give special thanks to Patricia Fripp, CSP, CPAE. Patricia has won or has been awarded every designation given by NSA, including their Hall of Fame, and their highest honor, the Cavett Award, which is considered the "Oscar" of the speaking world.

Thank you to those NSA members who contributed content to this book: Janelle Barlow, Ph.D., CSP, Art Berg CSP, CPAE, Jeff Blackman, J.D., CSP, CPAE, Roger E. Herman, CSP, CMC, Willie Jolley, CSP, CPAE, Lorna Reilly, CSP, Grady Jim Robinson, CSP, CPAE.

We also owe a special thanks to our clients who teach us as we teach them.

Dr. Michael Soon Lee, CSP
Bill Cole, MS, MA

Dedication

Free To Fee is dedicated to all the professional speakers in the world, and to those speakers who want to join their ranks. It is also dedicated to the people professional speakers serve, their audiences.

What Is Not In This Book

This book shows you how to make the transition from free or low-paid speaking to paid or professional speaking. This career shift requires a huge, multifaceted skill set. This book focuses mainly on the career strategies and daily, weekly and monthly tactics that help you navigate this undertaking. We cover the nuts and bolts of what you need to know in terms of career strategies, business skills, platform skills, topics, product development, fee setting, knowledge of how the professional speaking world works and inside tips from established speaking professionals.

In our next book we may cover some of these topics:

1. The executive who speaks.
2. Speaking for association and business audiences.
3. Practicing a speech.
4. Writing articles for ezines, newsletters, magazines and newspapers.
5. Getting media attention.
6. Working with speakers bureaus.
7. Using Toastmasters as a launching pad.
8. Setting up a website and blog.
9. Doing teleseminars and webinars.
10. How to create a demo video.
11. How to be a panelist and master of ceremonies (MC).

12. Print vs. digital marketing materials.
13. Back-of-room sales.
14. How to get income from no-fee engagements.
15. How to get a corporate sponsor.
16. Creative negotiating tactics for compensation.
17. Using barter and trade-outs.
18. How to speak on cruise ships.
19. How to handle stage fright.
20. Using high tech in presentations.
21. Using props in presentations.
22. Technical considerations when speaking.
23. Hiring a virtual assistant.
24. Hiring and using salespeople.
25. Doing seminars vs. workshops.
26. Setting up your business structure.
27. Accepting credit cards and PayPal.
28. Copyright and legal issues in speaking.
29. Contracts.
30. Public relations and promotions.
31. How to get testimonials.
32. Travel issues.
33. Speaking internationally.
34. How to set up a mastermind group.
35. Traditional book publishing vs. self-publishing.
36. Creating and using ezines, newsletters and mailing lists.
37. E-commerce shopping carts.
38. Appearing on TV, radio and podcasts.

What additional topics would you like to see us cover? Drop us a line and let us know.

How To Use This Book

We wrote this book so you can use it as your personal guide to the world of professional speaking.

This book does not need to be read in a linear manner from start to finish. Feel free to jump around and explore areas that you need right now.

Since we had a mentoring relationship when we began this book, we kept that flavor by using a question-answer format.

Within each chapter you may want to first scan the questions and simply read only those answers that you need right now.

The appendices contain specialized content that take a deeper dive into areas that professional speakers need to know and master.

Some of the documents in the appendix are interactive checklists you can use for your speaking engagements.

There is a glossary of terms used in professional speaking that are very handy to know. You'll use these all the time. Many people like to start here and get a sense of what is to come in the various chapters.

Introduction

This book is focused on helping you move from unpaid speaking into the world of professional speaking.

If you have a passion for speaking, can deliver on stage, are committed to continuous improvement, and can learn the business, the speaking industry can bring you untold joy and rewards. You can change people's lives.

Perhaps you are already a reasonably accomplished speaker, but you rarely get paid to speak. Maybe you're a local speaker who only gets trinkets, mugs, plaques and handshakes after each speech. You might be a speaker who has evolved into being awarded small "honorariums" that barely pay your travel and other speech preparation expenses. You could be a "part-time professional speaker" who is not speaking very often, and who still has a "day job". You might even be a full-time professional speaker-writer-consultant who speaks very little.

If you identify with any of these categories, you are reading the right book.

What's In This Book

This book is packed with more than 185 answers to the most vital need-to-know questions you have about professional speaking. There are specialized chapters on marketing, platform skills, setting fees, choosing topics and developing products. You'll learn how to work with meeting planners, understand attendees, write a speech, create a speaking contract, and understand how to move up in this business. You'll find examples of one sheets, resources for training and professional development, a speaking program equipment checklist, a pre-program letter to attendees, a speaking date action checklist, and a presentation analysis chart. Overall, there are hundreds of strategies and insights about the world of professional speaking you can put to immediate use. You can take strategies from any chapter or section and apply them to your business right now. You can use Free To Fee as a reference book as you build your speaking business.

Major Themes Of This Book: Marketing And Performance

Most books on public speaking focus on the actual skills of giving speeches. They talk about how to write a speech, practice it, deliver it, and how to improve your vocal skills and choreography on stage. Free To Fee focuses some on public speaking skills, and more about the business, products and career aspects of speaking.

Even though the public believes the core skills that professional speakers focus on the most are their platform skills, in reality, it is marketing and creating product that consumes professional speakers time the most. Our three longest question-answer chapters are Platform Skills, Marketing and Developing Product.

My Background

I taught college at three universities across the US for 15 years and had extensive classroom and convention speaking experience during those years. I taught stress management, teacher education, coach education and human development. I taught in human performance departments and physical education departments.

I actually gave my first "paid speech" in 1974, as an undergraduate when I was asked to teach a class in sport psychology for my professor, who was out of town. I was a college junior (age 19) and got $25, a sum that made me think, "This isn't too bad." I became hooked on speaking and regularly spoke at colleges on sport psychology, and at professional academic conferences. I owned a seminar business in the 1970's, doing "Zen Tennis" workshops and then again in the 1980's doing them for tennis and golf, which I still do today. I left the professional speaking game for about eight years and then returned to it in the early 1990's. I joined the National Speakers Association (NSA) in 1996.

During many of these years I was also a college tennis coach and tennis pro and owned tennis academies and camps, so I spoke at those venues daily. I started teaching tennis at age 15 and ½ and had led classes of all sizes in tennis instruction for over 25 years by the time I began in NSA. All of that regular teaching gave me confidence and skills as a speaker.

I owned a seminar business with my speaking topics focused on my brand, the mental game. I had programs for tennis players, golfers and many other sports. My sports clients eventually asked me if I could teach these same principles for their businesses, such as peak performance in sales, and to overcome stage fright in public speaking. I said yes, and new divisions of my business were born. I started to see brand new applications of my mental game theme, and I began to widen it to customer service, stress, teambuilding, leadership and communication. I also developed a special niche as an interview coach from my extensive experience being interviewed by the media.

The Struggling Years

Before Michael and I met I was speaking throughout California and occasionally nationally. I was not charging very much money. Definitely not enough money to make a living as a professional speaker. I was also doing a fair amount of free speaking to build up my contacts and to polish my delivery.

I did not yet have a website. I was just learning about the internet, speaker marketing and what the big world of "pro speaking" was all about. Even though I was a good, experienced speaker, I knew very little about what it took to succeed in paid speaking.

I was speaking regularly, while teaching college classes at San Jose State University and running my tennis academy in Saratoga, California. My two "day jobs" were very good, but they kept me so busy that I didn't have the ideal amount of time to put into professional speaking.

In the true pro speaking world, gigs were far and few between. I was speaking for pay about ten times a year. Like many people at my level, many gigs were often freebies to generate leads and testimonials. I was charging around $500-$1,000 for a 60-90 minute talk.

I really wanted to speak more, to charge more, and to deeply understand the pro speaking business so I could really make my speaking take off.

So when I met Michael, and we began our mentoring relationship, my speaking business really started to grow.

How Michael Lee And I Met

I was a member of the National Speakers Association (NSA). I was already a full professional member, so I was making some money in the industry. I was also a member of an outside professional speaker mastermind group comprised of fellow NSA-ers, and one day at that group mastermind meeting one of the members arranged for a speaker to come over and tell us about his pathway to becoming a CSP (Certified Speaking Professional), a designation from NSA. That speaker was Michael Lee. Michael was kind enough to spend time with us and to outline how he did it, and how we could too.

After Michael's talk I was very appreciative and told Michael how grateful I was that he took the time to come speak to us. He spent additional time with me in the parking lot answering my questions. Later that day I also sent Michael a nice email, thanking him again for his time and expertise. Michael replied that if I had any further questions, to email him. I did have additional questions over the next few days and Michael was kind enough to answer them all, with very good detail. I again told Michael how much I appreciated his efforts and diligence. In the next email, Michael told me that he would like to mentor me. He said he saw some good potential in me as a professional speaker. I thanked him, and our mentoring relationship was launched.

How This Book Came About

Our mentoring relationship continued for over a year. Then one time, after we had sent a flurry of emails back and forth, I said, "With all this great content, we should write a book!". Michael almost immediately said, "That's a great idea. Let's go for it!". And this book was born.

The start of our book happened in 2001. Fast forward to 2017. Only now is this book finally being published. What happened over those missing 16 years?

Well, a lot! Michael and I continued our book project. It evolved and expanded, dramatically. In fact, we had so many big ideas for making the book so different and special that we bit off more than we could chew, and we got bogged down. Eventually our ability to manage the project effectively decreased, and this project slipped into the shadows. We still had the best of intentions, and we kept working at it, but at a greatly reduced pace. With both our speaking schedules, our other business interests, and family and life events, the book project gradually ground to a halt on its own. We never officially called a stop to it. It just ceased to be a weekly priority. Over the years I would pick it back up at times, only to feel pretty overwhelmed at the enormity of our plans. It again went back into hibernation.

Now, in 2017, I've taken a different tack. I've cut back on some of our more grandiose plans for the book and made it more streamlined. That helped greatly reduce the time and complication factors. I found a wonderful book designer-publisher and she is helping shepherd the book through all the complex publishing labyrinths.

Where I Am Now

My frequency of paid speaking rose dramatically as a result of our mentoring. I spoke far more often, for better and larger clients, across the full range of pro speaking, and for higher fees. My current fee for a keynote program is $6,500 for 90 minutes. I developed a training business in Silicon Valley and also have a coaching division in a variety or areas, all with the theme in peak performance, the mental game.

I ultimately decided that the full-time world of professional speaking was not for me. I still speak nationally, and occasionally internationally. When I played college and pro tennis I traveled a lot, and I eventually realized that such extensive travel was not what I wanted any longer. So I could reduce travel I developed a thriving international membership, training and certification business that I could operate from by video from my offices in California, the International Mental Game Coaching Association:

www.mentalgamecoaching.com

When I started out in professional speaking years ago I had just a couple of programs. Today my mental game brand cuts across a number of program offerings:

www.mentalgamecoach.com/Services/SpeakingAndTrain ing.html

I became pretty well-known in the media as a mental game coach, and eventually got a call from Hollywood to fly down to shoot a series of TV pilots:

www.mentalgametvshow.com

I've even appeared in a film as a sport psychologist:

www.mentalgamecoach.com/BillColeOnTVRadioAndFilm.
html#BillColeInFilm

Even though professional speaking is still a big part of
what I do, it's not the only thing. In my sport
psychology practice, I write, teach, coach, create and
sell products and consult:

www.sportspsychologycoaching.com/aboutBillCole.html

I have a different set of offerings in my corporate
company:

www.mentalgamecoach.com/Products.html

How Michael's Mentoring Helped Me

Michael's mentoring cut years off my learning curve, and
saved me a huge amount of lost time and frustration. He
helped me to stop spinning my wheels. He helped me
avoid going down blind alleys and wasting energy and
focus that would have delayed my success. I saw my
speaking colleagues, who did not have access to this
specialized wisdom, becoming frustrated. Many dropped
out of the business, or had far less success than they
could have had.

What The Future Looks Like, My Goals

I will continue to develop new speaking and training
programs, and I will keep creating books, audios and
videos. In fact, I am dedicated in the near future to
producing a huge number of products that can help
people.

What Is Coaching And Mentoring?

Michael and I had a fantastic mentoring relationship.
Coaching is usually a one on one, paid process of a
coach imparting knowledge and skills to a learner.
Mentoring is usually more of an informal, unpaid process
of a person being a consultant or a career guide to a
person. These often turn into friendships.

How To Find And Work With A Mentor

We strongly recommend that you find a mentor in this business. The industry is too complicated to figure it all out on your own. Here are some guidelines that can help you find and work with a mentor.

1. Meet as many experts in your field as you can.

2. Arrange informational interviews with them. Don't ask to be mentored at first. Don't take too much of their time. Show sincere interest in what they are doing and show appreciation to them for their time and advice.

3. Allow the relationship to develop over time. It's important to find the right chemistry. You need someone you respect, admire and who has done what you want to do.

4. Think about how you would like a mentor to help you. What specifically can they help you with? How do you want that to transpire? In person? By phone or video? By email? How often do you want to contact the mentor?

5. Continue to show how grateful you are for their help. You aren't paying the mentor, so much of their motivation in the relationship is to watch you grow and to be a part of that cool process. Nurture it with gratitude.

6. Sometimes, after you have a few meetings with this special expert, they may ask you if you are interested in a mentoring relationship. Other times, you may have to ask.

7. Be open-minded on how the relationship will evolve. Be flexible with their needs and constraints. Remember, they are doing you a favor.

How Mentoring Cuts The Learning Curve

Most speakers who want to make money in this business toil for many years and use the trial and error method to learn what they need to know. This is a tenuous process at best. There is just too much to learn in this complicated industry, and the learning curve is too steep. By the time you know what you're doing, it's almost too late.

How This Book Can Help You

This book goes beyond most traditional books on learning how to become a speaker. Most such books delve very little into the business side of speaking. They focus on platform skills and how to write speeches, but not the nuts and bolts of setting up and operating a real speaking business. Free To Fee gives you the inside track on the business, since both authors have been in the industry a long time.

This book can help kick-start your entry into the world of professional speaking. It has the questions you've always wanted to know about this unique world, and the direct, hard-hitting answers from speaking pros. Some books on presentation skills might have a chapter or a few small passages about professional speaking, but the focus of Free To Fee is all about showing you how to transition from free or part-time paid speaking to full-time professional speaking.

How We Wrote This Book

We wrote this book virtually 100% via email. We rarely had very many face-to-face meetings since we didn't live very close to each other. We also did not have the need. Email was a very efficient process. We took a close look at the full breadth of the speaking business and decided to include only the core material we felt you needed to know right away. We wrote this material for your career level. These strategies can be used at any career level, but the major thrust of our content is aimed at the emerging speaker. We found that our email mentoring relationship was a fast-moving, efficient method of getting a lot done fast. We figured since that was optimal for us, it would also be good for our readers. So we decided to make seven chapters in a question-answer format. The other parts of the book are written in traditional book format, with other documents, such as the speaking contract and PPQ, in their original form. We both use many checklists in our speaking business, so we wanted you to see some of those as well.

Since Michael had been a CSP (Certified Speaking Professional, a designation from the National Speakers Association, NSA) for some time, we decided to send out emails to some of his fellow CSP colleagues in NSA to ask if they would be interested in contributing tips to our book. Many said they loved our book project, but that they were too busy to sit down to write. Many of them sent us multiple tips and strategies. We have included nine CSP's in this book. We are very appreciative to each of them.

Is Professional Speaking your Calling?

Professional speaking is not for everyone. A good test to see if it is for you is to ask yourself the question, "If I was not paid to speak, would I still speak?". If the answer YES! comes from deep within you, then you know you need to be a professional speaker. You see this business as more of a calling or a mission you are on. You view it as your destiny to change lives. You know that, even though this business calls for hard work, you are gladly dedicated to that hard work. You see it as a joy, and you're excited about the legacy that you'll leave to your audiences.

Michael and I hope this book inspires you to take your speaking career to new levels. We would love to hear from you as you progress. We wish you the best of luck, and know that you will find the professional speaking world to be exhilarating, rewarding and a never-ending learning experience.

" " Quotes On Speaking

Always be shorter than anybody dared to hope.

Lord Reading

Oratory is the power to talk people out of their sober and natural opinions.

Joseph Chatfield

Speaking before a group of strangers can be intimidating, but keep focused on the positive impact the presentation will have on your business reputation and your bottom line. Don't expect to be a magnificent speaker the first time out. Your goal is to present the most valuable information possible to the members of the audience. Think of it as the beginning of many long-term relationships.

Patricia Fripp, CSP, CPAE, Cavett Award winner

The World Of Speaking

Why do you want to be a professional speaker? Fame? Money? Travel? To help others? To spread your message? Are you naturally entertaining? Can you persuade people? Are you a talented teacher? If you have a desire to be in front of audiences where you can help improve their lives, there is a place in the speaking world for you. You don't need to be a Hollywood-style entertainer, a brilliant humorist, or an engaging storyteller to succeed in this business. Of course all those skills help! All you really need is the deep passion to be a change agent and to learn the speaking skills and business skills that will assist you in being effective with varying groups of people.

If you have that burning desire to share with others what is inside you, professional speaking is for you. If you know you have valuable content that can help others, you should be on stage. If your audience thinks differently, feels differently or behaves differently at the conclusion of your presentation, you have done your job as a speaker. You've made a difference in their lives. If you have a solid work ethic, want to learn every day, and have a positive, can-do attitude, you will do well in this business. This chapter gives you some insights into how you can find your niche in this industry.

1. What are the most pleasurable parts of the speaking business?

I hope I haven't made professional speaking sound too onerous! While it does take hard work and is less glamorous than it seems on the surface, there are many enjoyable aspects to the profession. Otherwise I, and many others wouldn't keep doing it.

I personally enjoy seeing parts of the U.S. and the world I might not otherwise get to visit. Many times we visit historic and interesting places in America and overseas locations, such as New Zealand, England, France, South America and the Caribbean. If you plan it right you can stay a couple of extra days in a nice place and play tourist. Another big attraction to professional speaking is meeting interesting people from all over the country and around the world. I try to meet for dinner with the more select organizers or participants. This way I get to learn how other people live and make new friends. I think a lot of us enjoy meeting the challenge of providing creative solutions to unique problems through a keynote or seminar. You've got to like this part of speaking or you won't last!

Then there's the ego gratification of being able to motivate and connect with audiences. There is little satisfaction comparable to being able to hold a large audience in the palm of your hand and give them a unique benefit like no one else can. Lastly, the money can be a satisfying reward for the ungodly hours, long flights, lonely travel and intense research required in professional speaking. I think the reason that we are often paid in the top one percent of people in this country is based on the unique value we provide.

2. How are speaking and training different?

Speaking is considered more motivational and emotion-driven as opposed to more content-rich training programs. I think what has made me successful is that I have found a way to be motivational even in very long training seminars. I find that it really helps to keep participants' attention and makes the learning much more enjoyable.

3. What differences are there between a seminar and a workshop?

Seminars tend to be more one-way from the speaker to the audience. Workshops tend to be more interactive with role-plays, group discussions and the like. However, these terms are often used interchangeably.

4. Do you subscribe to the often-heard bromide, "The speaking business is easy to get into, but hard to stay in"? Why is this?

I agree. Many people luck into the business such as instant celebrities with a book or event that makes them famous temporarily. I could name a lot of people but Scott O'Grady comes to mind. He's the US Air Force pilot who got shot down in the Middle East war and eluded capture for a week, then was rescued. He talks about his story, but now that the Gulf War is a distant memory he will have to find something else to talk about.

The same is true for all of the people who spoke about Y2K. What are they going to talk about now? As for me, the cultural thing will last a while but I'm already positioning myself in other areas. My next book is on the future of the service industries. I hope it will position me as more of a futurist.

5. What is "the speaking lifestyle"?

Professional speaking is a lot more rigorous than most casual observers think. Most people are only aware of the time a speaker is presenting at a program. After all, it doesn't seem so hard to get up and talk and get paid huge sums of money. Little do they know!

First, there's the travel. It's funny, but speakers are usually not perceived to be very highly valued until they leave their home state, which means to be successful you will probably have to travel a great deal. I have often spoken in five cities in five days across four times zones and have seen five hotels and as many as eight airports during that time. In one week of speaking I spent a total of 37 hours traveling, including cabs, limos, jets, prop planes, and private cars. Next, there's the constant research to keep topics current or to locate new hot subjects for programs. Finally, there's the continuous marketing that must be conducted to keep a speaker booked. Not an easy, luxurious lifestyle.

The good news is that with good planning and a bit of luck, you can see the world and meet some of the most interesting people in it. Over the past couple of years I have been fortunate enough to be able to visit: Mount Rushmore, the Rock and Roll Hall of Fame, attend a service in Martin Luther King's church, the Country and Western Hall of Fame, the Washington Monument, the Queen Mary, Graceland, Disney World, Hoover Dam, the Alamo, Pearl Harbor, and much more. While I often complain about the travel, I wouldn't give up the world of professional speaking for anything else.

6. Is it best to be an independent speaker or work for a company?

Many professional speakers start out working for seminar companies, presenting pre-written programs to pre-arranged audiences. While the pay is usually at the lower-end of the scale for speakers, it's great experience and you don't have to worry about marketing, coordinating meeting room facilities and making travel and hotel arrangements. When you become independent you have to pay for all of your marketing and make all of your own arrangements. If you're not careful you could end up netting less money after expenses as an independent speaker than you could working for a seminar company.

7. What breaks or opportunities should a newer speaker be watching for as they climb the ladder of success?

You should speak as often as you can even though it may be for little money or even for free. I'm a firm believer in making your own luck and the more people you speak to the more likely you are to be hired. These people can also give you valuable feedback about your presentation skills and program content.

As a speaker becomes more popular he must continuously look for ways to improve and add value to his programs. By eating with participants during lunch or dinner I often get priceless information about changes taking place in companies and industries. I will often change tables with each course to be able to speak with as many people as possible.

As you get more bookings, look for opportunities to increase your fees. Set a limit on the maximum number of programs you are willing to present each year. Once you hit your ceiling, raise your fees 10-15 percent. Yes, you will lose some clients but you'll probably make the same amount of money due to the fee increase. When you reach your maximum number of programs again at the higher fee, raise it again and start all over. No one starts out commanding fees of $10,000 or $15,000 a program. They have paid a lot of dues to get to that level.

Don't forget that a speaker's only value lies in the uniqueness of his or her program and in the contacts he or she has developed over the years. If you ever want to retire as a professional speaker you must have a current, computerized list of clients. Everything else, from your style to your content can be duplicated overnight, but not your client list.

8. Since you've been in the speaking business, what are your biggest surprises about the business itself that you did not know when you were on the outside looking in? What did the speaking business look like when you were on the outside, but now that you are in it, you know better?

I didn't know there was so much work involved BEFORE the speaking engagement. Talking to key people in companies to customize a seminar or keynote, rewriting my notes, redoing handouts, etc. takes a lot of time. When you see a speaker on stage all you see is the final product. You don't know how much work was done before. Patricia Fripp is legendary for her work before a program. Of course, the audience does not see or appreciate that.

9. For most speakers, what are the highest sources of stress?

I can't speak for other speakers. For me it's getting to the hotel from the airport! It's easy for me to get to the airport and deal with the flying, but finding my way out of a strange airport to an unfamiliar hotel or convention center is extremely stressful. From now on I am having a local person meet me at the gate and drive me to the speaking site or hotel regardless of how close it may be. It always takes 45 minutes to an hour to get to most airport hotels. The other things about speaking such as being in front of the audience, developing unique programs and writing books is relatively easy for me.

10. Have you ever looked into speaking on cruise lines? Are these any good? Is it a rite of passage for speakers?

I've already conducted seminars at sea in the Caribbean. I'll have to tell you some of my stories about trying to teach a group in 20-foot swells! It's very difficult to get a paying trip at sea. I was lucky. Most cruise lines give you a free berth and food. Airfare, transfers, and land tours are not usually paid. Also, you need to have a very generic program that appeals to a wide audience for them to want to book you. Having a book doesn't hurt either.

11. Does anyone start out as a keynoter? That seems to be what everyone seems to want the most.

Very few speakers begin as keynoters. That's because the pressure is greater there, the competition is greater and the skills required to grab and hold and entertain an audience are more sophisticated. For most speakers, it takes many years of diligent work to transition into keynoting. Most speakers begin as seminar leaders or workshop speakers.

12. Are keynoters the stars of the speaking world?

Trainers don't think so! Actually, it does seem that keynoters gather a larger share of the glory, particularly at conventions, but trainers and workshop and seminar speakers can be famous in their own ways, in their own markets. Keynoters are usually paid more per speech and speak to larger audiences than any other type of speaker. So for those reasons, I would have to say that it is generally seen that keynote speakers are "at the top" of the profession.

13. Are the platform skills different for a seminar speaker, workshop speaker, facilitator and keynoter?

We can say that speaking skills apply to every type of speaking situation, but keynoting is different from the others. A keynoter usually requires a very strong ego, and is someone who loves the spotlight.

However, there are well-known and successful keynoters who are actually rather shy "in real life". Generally, keynoters are more extroverted and love being on stage. The staging skills are different for keynotes and the speaking technique is different. Each of these styles has unique skills that are required to be successful. For example, a workshop leader needs to be able to interact with the audience, and to orchestrate their interaction with each other. A facilitator must have great listening and people skills and be able to limit their ego involvement in the proceedings.

14. Does everyone in professional speaking eventually become a keynoter?

Not everyone. Many speakers remain in the role of trainer, seminarian or workshop leader their entire careers. Some really just don't have the desire to become a keynoter. And that's OK. There's a place for everyone in this business.

15. What are some common misconceptions newer speakers have about the business?

Many new speakers believe the business is easy and that they'll immediately zoom right to the top. Little do they know about all the hard work that successful speakers must do to sustain their level of achievement. Many newer speakers are surprised to learn how long it takes to develop a signature speech. Others are surprised at the variety of skills required to start and maintain a professional speaking business. They see a professional speaker on stage and think that's what its all about—the glory. The biggest hidden part is probably the constant marketing and travel. As the saying goes, we're not in the speaking business. We're in the marketing of speaking business.

16. Should a new speaker expect to have a linear, fast rise to the top of this industry?

In a word, no. I've rarely seen this in all my years in the business. Does anyone start out in any industry at the top? No. They have to work their way up. There are many challenges and potential roadblocks that need to be overcome. It's not easy, but it's worth it.

17. Who makes the most money in this business? Keynoters? Trainers? Workshop speakers? Seminarians? Facilitators?

People can make money many different ways in this industry. People put together many different combinations of what you list here, and others like to specialize. Probably most professional speakers have done a little bit of everything along the way until they find what they like, and what they are good at. There is public speaking, speaking for corporations, for associations, for non-profits, for the academic market, for governmental entities and more. Each market has its own price structure. Professional speakers do well in all these venues.

18. Can a college professor or high school teacher transition well into professional speaking?

Yes, in fact teaching is an ideal launching profession for this business. Think of it. As a teacher or professor you are up in front of a classroom, on your feet, speaking often. You are a content expert, teaching people about a subject matter area in which you are an expert. This is how professional speaking is as well. Many professional speakers are former teachers. Some still teach at colleges and in other venues. Professional speakers have come from all walks of life, and from all educational backgrounds. There are no limits as to who can become a professional speaker. That is the beauty of this industry. The only limit is your talent, drive and creativity.

19. If a person has no background in speaking or teaching, can they still make it as a professional speaker?

Absolutely. I know professional speakers who have limited educational backgrounds, but who have tremendous life experiences that audiences want to hear about. They have no degrees in teaching or education. Of course, every speech we give has elements of teaching in it. If you are a trainer, you are teaching

29

more than you would be if you are a keynoter. Keynoting is more about entertaining, with some educational content.

20. I see at many of the NSA and other professional speaking conventions that most of the speakers are more middle aged and beyond. Is there a place in professional speaking for young speakers in their twenties?

Yes. There are professional speakers in their early twenties. They may be specializing in the teen, high school or college markets, but they do very well. They may also be former professional athletes who now speak. There are speakers at every age level.

21. How many years does it take to "make it" in this business?

That's different for everyone, but there are very, very few "overnight successes" in this business. About the only folks who catapult to success are those who were already famous, or became famous for something, and decided to capitalize on it. The vast majority of professional speakers simply work at their craft and the business for many years before they see consistent success. Of course, another way to view it is that no one ever really "arrives" in this business. That's a dangerous mindset. You're better to view yourself as a work in progress.

" "
Quotes On Speaking

Find out what's keeping them up nights and offer hope.
Your theme must be an answer to their fears.

Gerald C. Myers

The success of your presentation will be judged not by
the knowledge you send but by what the listener
receives.

Lilly Walters

Practice does not make perfect. Perfect practice makes
perfect.

Lorna Riley, CSP

Getting Started

Wisdom usually comes to those who have spent a long time in their chosen field, or to those who have made many fast, early mistakes. This chapter helps you cut your learning curve dramatically, by quickly learning about the mistakes most beginning speakers make so you can avoid them. There are many false pathways in this industry, and many things look one way, but they are really another. In fact, this business looks very easy from the outside looking in. All professional speakers have made mistakes along the way. Our goal here is to spare you some pain from all-too-easy-to-make errors so you can move ahead in your career faster. It's usually very insightful to ask an experienced speaker about what they wished they knew about the industry when they started out. There are strategies that emerging professional speakers should specifically use, and we lay them out for you here.

1. What are the "hidden pitfalls" that starting speakers don't know about in the business that can sink a career fast? I've heard major mistakes can kill a career almost overnight.

These are all things for new speakers to avoid.

1. Poor cash flow. You need savings to get through the slow times. There are peaks and valleys in speaking. At the peaks you can't spend the money like it's going to continue forever, because it won't. Savings will take care of the valleys.

2. Poor business management. Always remember that this is a business and must be run like one. Start with a business plan that includes a budget for marketing and staffing. Track all of your income and expenses.

3. Stealing people's material. It's hard to be original at the beginning. New speakers don't even know who they are yet, so they adopt other people's styles. This is OK. Taking their material is not. However, anyone is welcome to my material. If that's all I am then I don't have much. They still won't have my delivery, style or knowledge behind the words. That's the real difference between any of us in the long run.

4. Growing too big too fast. Not a problem if you have a business plan. Just watch the cash flow.

5. Bombing in front of an important, influential audience. We all have bad days. Great speakers will bomb but still get good marks from the majority. The biggest danger is speaking in front of the wrong audience.

6. Upsetting the wrong people who hold power in the business. Sometimes this is necessary to make changes. You just have to use common sense and not burn bridges.

2. Any other pitfalls?

I think the biggest danger for starting speakers is not being open to learning. We all want to think we are the best at what we do, but there is always someone else who is better. I go out of my way to watch people like Patricia Fripp, Brian Tracy, Wayne Dyer, and others. I have worked for free to be able to get back stage at large teleconferences just to see how it's done. I'm still learning and will continue to do so until the day I die. We need to surround ourselves with people who will tell us that we are NOT perfect. Those who will tell us the truth about us, and not just tell us how great we are. We need to cultivate an atmosphere of openness among our friends and peers if we are ever going to be the people we want to be.

3. Should I target key service clubs in high-potential areas that have members that can hire me? If so, what would your opinion of the premium ones be?

Exactly. Start with Rotary and then work your way through the "animal" clubs. The animal club circuit is the Lions, Elks and Moose Lodge organizations that bring in speakers for free or very low fee. You get to practice in your own backyard, under low-pressure conditions. You can try out new material.

4. Should I do the same for Chamber of Commerce meetings?

Yes, but in the same cities above. Go for the largest audiences. Ask the Rotary and chamber of commerce which are their largest branches.

5. What do you think about the following to gain some "name clients"? I'll do my "trade freebie" program to local branch offices or locations of well-known national businesses? I think these would be easy to book via my above program, and they could lead to something.

A local store of Office Max or Office Depot

A local store of Burger King or Mc Donald's

A local car dealership of a national franchise

Maybe one or two for each but not more. After that you want a referral to the regional sales manager.

6. As a starting speaker, what do you recommend as the most important steps to take at the beginning?

Join a group like Toastmasters or the National Speakers Association. They can help assess where you are now and assist you in getting to the next level in your speaking career. These groups will save you hundreds of hours because they will keep you from making basic mistakes that many beginning speakers make. Then develop a unique niche or topic and take it on the road. Speak for free if you must to improve your speaking skills while refining your topic.

7. What are the errors a starting speaker can make that can sink a career fast?

Not trying out your topic in front of non-threatening audiences. Not learning and doing marketing. Not spending more time marketing than speaking. Giving up too easily.

8. Should my marketing plan be different from that of an established speaker?

No. There is very little difference in marketing for established and beginning speakers. Marketing is marketing except that established speakers may be able to afford to have someone else do much of the work.

The key to successful marketing at any level is to be consistent. Even established speakers who fail to regularly market to potential customers find themselves sitting by the phone waiting for it to ring. Do the kind of marketing you feel most comfortable with and keep improving it. Make your marketing materials look professional by hiring a graphic designer and purchasing a high quality color printer. Remember, it takes money to make money and speakers must continually market themselves.

9. How do I know when to quit my day job and begin speaking full-time?

Ideally, when you can earn as much from speaking as your regular job, it's time to make the change. However, in reality, it's hard to be away from your day job to speak enough to make enough to replace that income. Most speakers get to a point where they can see that if they quit their steady job they could survive and eventually surpass their former incomes.

Ultimately, it takes a leap of faith to become a full-time professional speaker. One week you could make $10,000 and then go a month or even several months without any paid engagements. Wait until you are getting fairly steadily booked before quitting your day job. Even if each speaking date doesn't pay that highly, it's easier to raise your fees than get additional bookings.

For those with less faith in their speaking abilities or who have high fixed expenses, you might want to consider taking a part-time job in real estate or bar tending at night to keep some income flowing while you transition to full-time speaking.

10. What is the National Speakers Association, and how can they help a new professional speaker?

NSA is the largest association of professional speakers in the world. Many people join so they can get booked as speakers, but this is a fallacy and a mistake. The members of NSA are a resource to help you get to the next level in your speaking career. There is information available on marketing, setting fees, content development, platform skills improvement, product development, and much more. The organization does not book speakers, however. As with any group, you only get as much value as you contribute. As people help you move up in your career, you will be asked to help others below your current level. I hope you will keep the speaking profession strong by giving back what you have received.

11. What is Toastmasters, and how can they help a new professional speaker?

Toastmasters helps people learn how to speak capably and confidently. This is an essential skill in business as well as in professional speaking. They also help members handle difficult audiences and to think one's feet. However, the main goal of toastmasters is not to get paid for speaking. Once one has developed confidence and skill at speaking then joining the National Speakers Association would be the next step to becoming a paid professional speaker.

12. I have a job teaching and training. Can that help me get into speaking?

Teaching and training are great ways to get paid to learn how to speak. However, they are not the same as speaking in front of paying audiences of strangers. You must transition from teaching and training to paid speaking by speaking for free at civic and other groups.

13. How many years does it take to get to the various levels in pro speaking?

It's hard to put any specific time frames to moving to the various levels of paid speaking. Some people can progress fairly quickly while others take more time. Unfortunately, professional speaking does not have a logical and predictable progression from one level to the next. However, groups like the National Speakers Association help speakers move from whatever level they happen to be at to the next level at their own rate.

14. How important is being motivated to succeed in professional speaking?

You must be motivated to succeed at anything but probably more so at professional speaking. This is because our profession is so competitive and demanding. It can be extremely discouraging to speak to a group for free and get absolutely no bookings from it. That's when motivation takes over and keeps you going when everyone and everything seems to tell you to quit. While speaking may seem easy, it is deceivingly difficult, which is why so few people are successful at it. Yet, some of us persist because we feel strongly that we have something of value to offer our audiences and feel compelled to present it in spite of the naysayers.

15. What have been your "big breaks" at each step of moving up the ladder?

I think breaks are the result of preparation meeting opportunity. I have done probably 50 programs for Coldwell Banker locally and internationally. They originally asked me to do one very small program for very little money. But I really showed them what I could do, and over time they've become a great client. It was the same thing for the National Association of Music Merchants. It took me three years to put together one small program on marketing for them. Now they have hired me to do at least 25 others. I will speak at least 10 times for them this year. In other words, I don't think I've had many breaks in the sense of big leaps in my career. I started out as a college teacher in 1981, became a trainer for the California Association of Realtors in 1991 for $700 a day, and kept increasing my programs and fees. The Realtor Association asked me to put together my first cultural program on Selling to Asian Real Estate Clients in 1992, but it wasn't until about 1995 that I really started concentrating on culture. That's when I began working on my CSP in earnest.

16. What would you identify as being your first real "big break" in the business?

My first break was in having my audiences force me to speak about cultural issues. Until then I tried to be all things to all people. If you wanted a time management seminar, motivational program, sales training, etc., I would do it. Now, everything emanates from my focus on cultural training. My seminars, books, website, etc. are all focused on helping people sell to people from other cultures. Again, after a group or company gets to know my abilities, they often ask me to do "non-cultural" programs including motivational keynotes. The key is getting your foot in the door with your specialty and then forcing it open with your talent.

17. What needs to be your next big break to move you where you want to be at the next level of success?

I would like to become a CPAE (Council of Peers Award of Excellence from NSA) but that is not something you can earn. You must be inducted from a panel of top professional speakers. I guess you just keep speaking and improving and maybe someone at national recognizes your success. If one of my future books became a best-seller it would certainly help my career! Again, that's not something that can be planned for. I'm just enjoying the progress I've made so far and looking for new opportunities. When you speak regularly other things open-up that are totally unexpected. I'm also keeping an eye out for subjects on which I can speak passionately. My next topic that seems to be developing is debunking the myth of the Internet. Everyone thinks it's the next "magic bullet" to success for retailers when it's really not. My next book will spend some time addressing this issue.

18. When it's all said and done, and your career is over, how will people remember Michael Lee, CSP? How do you want them to remember you?

I would like people to remember me as someone who cared about helping others. The time, effort, energy and emotion expended on speaking is certainly huge. However, if people are helped in reaching their goals by what I have given them, then I have been successful in my own eyes.

19. What niche and expert area do you see yourself evolving into?

I'm not sure. It depends on where the audience takes me. At every program I always talk to the audience and ask, "What issues keep you awake at night?" That led to my second most popular program, "Runnin' with the Big Dogs" on how to compete with larger competitors.

❝ ❞ Quotes On Speaking

All the great speakers were bad speakers at first.

Ralph Waldo Emerson

In oratory the greatest art is to hide art.

Jonathan Swift

Always remember to have fun and stay focused on inspiring the audience, and not just impressing them. Not only will it help you to be audience entered but it will take away a lot of your nervousness.

Dr. Willie Jolley, CSP, CPAE

Developing Unique Topics

It's vital that you develop your brand, at multiple levels. One major way you do this is to speak on special topics. You want to stand out and "be known" for a particular topic area. Specialists are sought out far more than generalists. They are also paid more. You don't want to be a jack of all trades and master of none. You want to be an expert and an authority.

Do competitor research in your topic area so you know what has already been done. Then do something different from them. You can get ideas from people in your niche, but don't copy them. You want to develop your "special sauce" so you are associated with that particular concept in your topic area. If you do this, you'll be seen as a customized speaker, rather than "off the rack", or one of many. Too many emerging speakers want to speak on their "passion area", but if this is an area with little demand, it's of no use. Many newer speakers may already be an expert in a topic area, and if they are somewhat tired of that niche, they will decide to speak on topics that are brand new to them, so they feel excited and can learn as they go.

This is usually a mistake, because audiences want to listen to experts, not someone who is learning on their dime. Speak in your sweet spot first, so you'll have instant credibility and depth of knowledge. You'll also be more comfortable on stage, since there would be very little your audience could ask you that you would not know. Later, you can expand into newer areas that interest you, as long as these topics fit your overall brand. Remember, think systematically with your brand at all levels. You can't go wrong.

1. Should speakers of all levels have a focus, or be generalists?

Unless you have the funds to market to everyone, it's best to start out speaking with a clearly-defined focus. For instance, I started out my career speaking to real estate agents on how to sell homes to Asian clients. Talk about a focus! However, what this did was enable me to easily, quickly and inexpensively target groups who would be likely to pay to hear my topic. All I had to do was to contact Boards of Realtors and large real estate companies in areas where large groups of Asians lived, such as San Francisco and Los Angeles. Once people there heard me speak they asked if I could present other topics of a more general nature, such as Marketing for Real Estate Agents and Time Management. My focused topic got me in the door; being good got me invited back to present other programs.

2. What tips do you have for creating book and program titles?

Look at the names of products on store shelves. The top selling bran flake cereal is called "Wheaties". The top selling toilet cleaner is called "Tidy Bowl". Your titles have got to grab the attention of readers and meeting planners. Play with your titles until they grab you. My first program was originally titled, "Selling Homes To Asians". Then it was "Why Don't They Do As Americans Do?" Now it's called "The Cultural Advantage".

3. What is a corporation or association "passion area"?

That's easy. Anything that will make them or their members money. By that I mean programs on sales and marketing are probably always going to be popular. Beyond that, you've got to read trade publications and association magazines for the topics that are currently hot for the groups you speak to. At the moment, quality of life in a hectic world is a big issue, but that could change tomorrow.

4. Should I offer one main program and have others under development?

You always want to be known by meeting planners and bureaus for one major topic. Otherwise there's no way they can remember you. However, you should always be looking for developing issues in the industries in which you speak. I always try to have lunch with attendees and ask them what subjects they would like to hear about. It gives me a sense of the ever-changing market in which I speak.

5. How many different programs should I offer at first?

It's probably best to only offer two or three programs. Otherwise, people wonder how you could possibly be an expert in a dozen or more expertise areas. It also confuses people that hire speakers to give them too many choices.

6. What level of customization do you typically do?

It depends on the program and the client. For a new client in a new industry, I will do more customization than a repeat client in an old industry. I always spend some time talking to key people about their needs, the solutions they have come up with, and obtain quotes. The client loves it.

7. Do you include comments from interviews of attendees?

Yes.

8. Do you put those into your workbooks?

Not usually. My workbooks are pretty generic, although a quote from the CEO is often used.

9. Do you use attendees' names and quotes?

Not in the workbook but in the program, yes.

10. Do you bring folks up on stage?

Sometimes, especially if they have a great story or example that I know in advance.

11. Do you interact with them in the talk?

Always, from the start and then throughout. What people like most about my programs is the ability to interact and ask questions. Remember, even the most difficult question can be answered with, "That's a great question, let me check my facts before I answer."

12. Do you put their data onto your slides?

Yes, and I even use their logo scanned into my computer.

13. How much customization would this be, from your off the shelf program?

Again, since quotes are not used in the workbooks there is not much difference. I just use their quotes instead of my quotes or someone else's.

14. Do speakers say they will customize and then just give the off the shelf program often? In other words, is the reality of it that no one really customizes to a very high degree?

I'm not sure. Every speaker claims to customize but few incorporate it into their program. Whether they don't do it or fail to mention it I don't really know.

15. At some level, do you customize and tweak your programs each time?

Yes, I think it makes the program better each time and keeps me interested. I also like to get quotes from people they might not normally think of like a parking lot attendant, heavy equipment operator, or janitor because they're all part of the company and part of the problem.

16. What type of multi-media stuff do you do in your programs?

Mostly PowerPoint presentations with scanned images or pictures to make it customized. I set the customized pictures in their own file so I can substitute them quickly for the next client. I sometimes add video and sound when appropriate. Remember, you want them to remember you--not your PowerPoint. Handouts are always very complete with references and my e-mail address so they will keep them and use them long after I'm gone.

17. What order do you use to create a program? (or tweak an existing one):

I start with:

- File folder full of ideas on the subject

- Write ideas in note form

- Do research to fill in any gaps

- Write ideas in note form

- Organize the notes into logical order

- Develop major subject headings

- Develop minor subject headings

- Develop student outline using major & minor subheads

- Use details to determine bullets

18. What is a speaker's "passion area"?

A speaker's passion area is a subject on which they would speak even if they weren't getting paid. For example, I would try to help others understand multicultural people like myself for free. It's important to me, and people like me.

You must have passion for your subject because you will spend an awful lot of time speaking on the topic, researching it and possibly even writing a book about it. Without passion for your subject, you will be a very unhappy and probably bitter person. This is not the clay of which great speakers are molded.

19. What is a "signature story"?

A signature story is one that you are known for. It is associated with you and you with it. People often think of my signature story as the one I tell about my dating experiences in high school. When a young lady would invite me to her parents' house, I knew that things were getting serious. However, if the parents were Chinese they would always ask me the same question, "What dialect of Chinese do you speak?" Many people know that I am a fifth-generation Chinese American and do not speak any Chinese. Thanks to the California public school system - I speak SPANISH! To tell an attractive girl's parents that I don't speak one of the proudest languages in the world would kill any chances I might have with their daughter. So what did I do? Like any red-blooded teenager--I lied. I picked the most obscure dialect of Chinese I could think of which was called "Fukienese". Most of the time the parents would frown and say, "That's too bad, we speak Cantonese or Mandarin". Then I would reply, "That's OK. We'll get by using English." This worked like a charm until I actually met a family with a daughter from Fukien and I was caught red-handed!

Many people are afraid others will steal their signature story but I'm not. As the only Asian American Certified

Speaking Professional in the National Speakers Association, who else could tell that story?

20. What is the "head message"?

The head message is the logical lesson you want to teach. For me the head message is usually, "Treat others as you would like to be treated". It's the academic part of your program.

21. What is the "heart message"?

The heart message is what you grab the audience's emotions with that can help cement the head message in their consciousness. My heart message is telling my audience how it feels to be called a "Ching Chong Chinaman" when you are only five years old, or how I've been discriminated against. It makes my head message more memorable.

" " Quotes On Speaking

Public speaking is an audience participation event; if it weren't, it would be private speaking.

Anonymous

A speech should not just be a sharing of information, but a sharing of yourself.

Ralph Archbold

Write a book, on-target with your expertise. The alignment between your writing and speaking will serve you well. Remember, the most successful speakers are experts who speak, not just speakers.

Roger E. Herman, CSP, CMC

Platform Skills

There are speakers who are energetic, charismatic rock stars when they take the stage. There are speakers who are low-key, solid and workmanlike. And there are speakers that fall in between this range. Regardless of style, a speaker must connect with their audience, and they must hold that connection. Every speaker needs that ineffable quality known as stage presence, or star quality. They need to often be "larger than life" to command respect from the audience. This chapter tells you how to grab and hold an audience, and what to do if that sometimes fragile connection begins to waver. We also tell you about the use of notes, how to open and close your talk, and how to handle questions from the audience.

1. What types of multimedia should I use in my programs?

Use whatever supports your presentation. Many times in my keynote I don't want anything to interfere with my personal connection with the audience. It's just me, a microphone and the audience. In longer programs I will use an overhead projector, a computer projector or just a flip chart to illustrate my points. A fancy multimedia show will not make a poor presentation good. It can sometimes actually be distracting, so I just use media to keep the audience on track with the outline during a long workshop or to emphasize a point. I sometimes use videotaped scenes from movies to make a point as well.

51

By the way, I paid for a license to play the movies. Speakers must be aware of copyright laws during their programs.

2. Should I memorize or use notes in my speech?

A keynote speech should be memorized. Don't commit it to memory□word-for-word but rather as actors do, scene by scene. It should be told as a story that flows naturally from point to point. For longer workshops, notes are generally acceptable. Attendees seem to prefer speakers who follow their outline and cover the material promised. Notes are a good way to make sure this happens. Again, don't read notes word-for-word-use them to make sure you cover the main points in each section you are discussing.

3. What is a close?

A close is the finish or ending to your speech or program.

4. What types of closes are there?

There are dramatic closes, question closes, answer closes, humorous closes, etc. There are as many different closes as there are different speakers. Close with what you want your audience to remember. It may be all that they take home even after an all-day workshop. I like to reinforce my main point by closing with a story.

5. I understand you acted in and produced major motion pictures. Was your acting training worthwhile?

As far as speaking, I'm not sure. It certainly helps you to command a stage, be more aware of your body and to capture the attention of the audience. I don't think it's essential for speakers. I've also trained at stand-up comedy, which helps with stage presence and timing. Speakers should take classes in almost all the performing arts if they want to be really good, including juggling and magic.

My favorite acting, however, is live stage where you must make an immediate connection with the audience and maintain it. This is very similar to speaking except in speaking there are no other actors to pick-up your lines if you forget one. There are no edits.

6. If the speaker does NOT grab them, is all lost?

Not lost, but the job is just much tougher. You will probably spend the rest of the program trying to recapture the rapport that could have been yours from the start. It also helps to tell a short but uniquely personal story about yourself. Nothing builds rapport more than letting people know you right from the start.

For example, in a diversity program I often will talk about the difficulties I've had relating to people from other cultures. Because I'm Asian, people usually find it hard to believe when I walk out on stage that I've ever had this problem, but I have.

For instance, when I was in high school I desperately wanted to be liked by girls (who didn't?) I really knew I was on the right track when a girl would invite me over to meet her parents.

Unfortunately, Asians are some of the most prejudiced people in the world. You wouldn't think so because we have very similar physical characteristics but they are. For instance, the Chinese will often shun those who don't come from the same village and speak the same dialect of which there are thousands.

Most of the girls I dated in high school were Chinese and the first question their parents would ask me was, "What dialect do you speak?" Now remember that I'm a fifth-generation Chinese American. In fact, my Great Grandmother, Jenny Kwok, was born in Monterey, California in 1886.

53

As a result of our long history in America, I speak NO Chinese. Why should I any more than any other European American?

If you know anything about the Chinese culture you know that they are extremely proud of this heritage and of the Chinese language. As a result, the first question Chinese parents would always ask me was, "What dialect do you speak?"

You must understand that for anyone of Chinese ancestry not to speak the language is to lose face or be shamed. In fact, the Chinese have a special word for American-born Chinese who cannot speak the language "jook sing" which literally means "empty head".

So, you can imagine what my future would have been with a young Chinese girl if I had told her parents that I didn't speak Chinese. So, like any normal red-blooded American teenager - I fibbed. Knowing that the most common dialects of Chinese Americans were Cantonese and Mandarin I tried to think of the most obscure dialect I knew which was "Foo Kien". Usually, the parents would say, "Oh, too bad. We don't speak your dialect." To which I quickly replied, "That's OK. We'll have to make do with English." However, every once in a while a girl's parents would actually speak Fookinese and I got caught in a lie. How embarrassing! So I know what it's like to be around people who speak a language we don't understand.

7. Can you or should you limit the number of questions the audience has so you can stay on time?

If they bog me down, I don't get to the workbook fully and people are disappointed.

8. Any other ways to allow all the questions, but still get to the entire content?

It depends on the program. Some programs will naturally elicit a large number of questions. I limit people to three questions. The audience is really good about telling the more aggressive students that they've used up their quota. However, normally, I plan enough time in my program for a standard number of questions. Then, I note in my outline where I should be at any particular time. If I get too far behind I ask them to hold questions to the end "Or else we'll have to stay past the promised finish time". They really get that and are very cooperative about it since they want to get out on time.

When you tell your audience how many breaks and when they will be, you are obliged to stick to it. It's a verbal agreement between the presenter and the audience. If you break too many of these promises you will lose their trust. This become crucial when you sell product at the back of the room.

9. How do you maintain the audience connection once you have it?

I'm very sensitive to audience energy and my connection to it. In fact, it feeds me when we are connected. If I sense that connection is waning or gone I will always go to an appropriate story about myself.

Presenting diversity programs is extremely difficult because there is so much built-in resistance to it by participants. Not only are there many people who just do not care about other people's differences, there are also those who think they could teach the class because they have lived the life of a minority in this country. While they may be able to retell incidents from their lives, they would have no idea how to get others to relate to them.

For instance, besides language, culture brings differences in beliefs, personal space and other aspects to the workplace. I will talk about how my beliefs have been impacted by my Chinese heritage as well as my American. I will explain that an American has beliefs such as the number 13 being unlucky. Then, I show them why many Asians have the same belief about the number 4. In fact, there are no fourth floors in hospitals in Asia. I tell them that this would be equivalent to being in intensive care on the 13th floor of a hospital here. One is not more right than the other. They are just different ways of believing in the same thing. When explained this way, people start to get interested in other people's beliefs.

10. What is taking command of the stage mean for a speaker?

Controlling everything that happens in front of the audience. Not only your body language and voice but creating an emotional bond with the audience so that they are open to accept the information you want them to have. Great speakers as well as entertainers can do this consistently regardless of their physical size. People like Sammy Davis, Jr. were masters at building and maintaining rapport with their audiences.

Part of the key to this, which is also known as charisma, is allowing yourself to be vulnerable to an audience. The average speaker is not comfortable enough to let their flaws show. People do not want to see perfection. They will only accept information that can change their lives from human beings who can relate to them.

I started my speaking career thinking I had to give a perfect performance. While these programs may have been technically superior to the ones I do today I don't believe they touched people and changed lives like the programs I share with audiences now. People remember those things which touch their hearts, not their heads. We can only touch people with our humanness.

11. Once you are introduced, and are walking to your "spot" to begin, when do you start talking?

This depends on the group. If it's a high-energy program I will start with something to pump them up like a cheer or ice breaker exercise. If it's a serious subject I will take a very long time before I start speaking. I will acknowledge applause, walk a bit and think, stop and then start very quietly. Then build to a climax which shows their need and promise to provide solutions.

12. Why is the initial first impression so important for a speaker to grab the audience?

Credibility and rapport are built in the first three minutes. This is not to say that if these are not done during this time they can never happen, but they will be much more difficult to build. You know what they say about never getting a second chance to make a good first impression.

Here are some ways to make a good first impression. Write out your introduction and print it in 14-point type minimum. Keep it short but make it impressive. Read it aloud to make sure it flows smoothly. Fax or e-mail your introduction to your introducer well in advance of your program. Have them run through it with you prior to the program. If there is no introducer, ask someone from the audience to introduce you. It is crucial to your credibility to have someone, other than yourself, introduce you. All of your accomplishments sound much more impressive and believable when coming from someone else. If possible, have the coordinator of the event or some other responsible and experienced person read the introduction. Otherwise, just pick someone who appears gregarious and ask them nicely. In a pinch, I will have an audience member read my bio right off the back jacket of my book. You can't believe how much credibility you gain when someone else holds up your book and reads your bio from it.

13. If the connection is lost, how can it be recaptured?

You must make a common connection from your background to theirs.

14. How long an opening do you recommend prior to digging into the workbook material? My intention in the opener is to set the tone, be humorous and make it OK for them to laugh, perhaps amaze them with a magic trick or two, get the energy up, tell a personal story that grabs them, and then "Tell them something they did not know that will blow them away." Anything you'd change in the above or add?

You want to get into the workbook within a few minutes, otherwise people will wonder why they have it. I would say no more than 10-minutes before at least getting into the first page. Then you can digress and come back. Don't forget that the open has to expose a need in the audience or they won't care about anything else. Remember, all they want to know is "What's in this for me?" You may also be trying to do too much with your open. The open should build credibility and introduce the need. Then get into the meat and then tell stories to cement them in the minds of the audience.

15. I tend to visually speak to or across the entire group with my gaze, rather than one person at a time sometimes. Other times I stop at one person, finish a thought and move to the next. How do you make eye contact?

Instead of gazing at corners of the room in a clockwise pattern, it's better to start and end a thought with one person. The people around them will think you are talking with them anyway and your connection will be better.

16. I like to use everything and everyone in the room to my advantage so I can play humor off of it. I will talk to the introducing person, the room monitors, the waiters, or anybody who can fit into the topic and add value, and to loosen up the audience. It fits my style, and in a more casual workshop it seems OK. Would this NOT be acceptable in a corporate seminar?

I would do less of it in a corporate seminar. It is not quite as relaxed and informal as a low-key workshop. Also, much of your humor may be pre-planned. There's plenty of things that will naturally happen in a program which will be funny - if you're open to it. It's really much funnier and more enjoyable for you when it comes as a surprise... to everyone.

17. If I'm giving a keynote from a lectern, is it OK to use notes, since they are "hidden"? Or in an hour keynote, should I just memorize it or use a brief memory outline, kept on the lectern?

Patricia Fripp walks in Golden Gate Park and memorizes a three-hour program that way. My memory is shot so rarely can I remember a new thirty-minute program much less a three-hour one. So I use an outline of the major points I want to make and memorize the modules. I then put the outline on the lecture and walk by it literally on the way to my next point. I've also hidden the notes on an empty chair in the front row or on the desk at the front of a classroom.

Beware though: One time I had some mischievous adult students deliberately mix my notes up just to see if they could throw me. Fortunately, I knew the material and covered that section from memory before putting them back into order. Actually, they were quite impressed but disappointed that their trick didn't have more dire consequences.

18. Any tips to save your voice over a long day of speaking?

I often put a sugar-free menthol cough drop in my cheek throughout a long program. In addition, I drink lots of water or "Throat Coat" tea if I need it. Protect your voice. It's all you've got. I often use a singing coach who can help me with projection and proper breathing. Speaking is much like singing.

19. How long should a close be?

The close should be short but should remind the audience of the main points you covered. Have a short saying that they can remember you by and build to a climax. For instance, my close for my multicultural seminar is, "I want to wish you the best of luck with all of your customers. No matter what country... or what planet they may come from."

20. Should the audience KNOW you are starting to close or should it gradually sneak up on them or should it suddenly end, leaving them in shock?

Don't say, "In closing". It's distracting. You want it to sneak up on them because your program is so good they think you are only going on hour two of your three hour program. You want them to say, "That was the fastest three-hours I've ever sat through!"

If you say, "In conclusion" they'll start looking for that section of the book or at their watch or think about where they parked the car. You want them to listen to your finish. If you do it right they'll instinctively know you are concluding.

21. With a new program, or with an established program you have, but that you are doing in a new time format, how do you time the day? If you have a 1/2 day program and the client wants a full day or half-day, how do you actually time the verbal program, the workbook length and the media and the questions so you hit the time mark?

It's hard. I always put more material into my program than I could ever deliver. That way I have to give it extra energy to even get close to covering the material. I don't put everything in the outline so people don't know when I'm skipping certain sections. Also, I always have "filler material" in my notes so I can stretch the program if necessary.

22. This is my toughest dilemma at the moment. It killed me to get the whole thing to come out in order and on time when I created it.

It takes practice. Even the pros don't usually get it right on the first attempt. Don't forget, even a perfectly-timed program (if there is such a thing) can be destroyed by an extremely inquisitive group. Do you want to sacrifice the connection to the audience to give them a couple of points they'll never remember anyway? Remember, becoming a great speaker depends on quality, not quantity.

23. What acting training have you undergone to date? Do people realize that you have that background when they hear you speak?

I studied at the American Conservatory Theater in San Francisco and at the Lee Strassberg Institute in Hollywood. No, I usually don't mention it unless it's appropriate.

24. How long is a good opening before you shift gears and get into the meat of the program? (Even though the opening should directly be the meat, otherwise why have it?).

It depends on the kind of program. If they want content you have to get into the meat right away and blow them away with at least one thing you know that they don't or you won't get their attention. This is particularly true for tech seminars. For after-dinner keynotes you can take your time. This is where experience comes in.

25. If you tell an opening story that impacts the reason for the program or sets the stage, how long would that be?

Again, it depends on the program and the story. If the story is really applicable you can take your time since it is part of the presentation. If just setting the tone, it should be short.

It also depends on what went on just before. For example, if there was a fun luncheon and you have a serious talk, it will take longer to change the mood.

26. Do you directly refer to the workbook as you go, by page number, or just let them read on their own?

I like to just give them a reference or two like "In Roman III ..." for those people who like to follow along. Otherwise you get dinged on your evaluations for "not following the outline".

27. How do you handle Q and A? Do you ever have a specific Q and A session at the end, or does" taking questions as you go" handle that?

Again, it depends on the program. If it's an interactive workshop, I take them as I go. If it's a keynote I hold them to the end so they can edit them out of the tape. If I'm in the middle of a thought I will ask them to hold it. People seem to really like the way I handle Q & A, which they seem to think is "fair and thorough".

28. In terms of closes, what do you suggest? I like to wrap the close to the opener or the day by telling a short inspirational story calling them to action to implement what we did all day.

This is great. You've got to remind them of one point they can take away. A story helps to cement it in their minds. I do the same.

29. Do you say, "to close".... or "finally"....or "now that our time is over"....and THEN tell the story, or just launch into it?

I don't say anything about the closing. Makes it seem contrived and breaks the mood. If you are "in the groove" they will sense it coming. I want to end with the audience saying, "Is that it? Seemed so short. Is that an hour already?"

30. As the final touch, after your closing story is over, etc. do you just say, "Thank You" and they applaud or do you bow? Do you hold your arms high? What signifies to them that it's over?

Although it's against the rule, I usually say, "Thank you" which gives them permission to applaud. Otherwise there is a hesitation that hurts the enthusiasm. I then nod at specific people and say. "Thank you" again. This is probably one of the most personal parts of the program-how people accept applause.

31. If you skip speaking to pages in the workbook, do they see that as a negative?

Sometimes, after doing the workbook or based on their needs, I like to skip a page or two in the moment, and select what I see as important.

My outlines aren't as extensive so they rarely see me miss anything since I only include the essentials. That way, when I give them more they see it as a bonus rather than a negative.

32. If you end up leaving out larger sections of the workbook, do they ding you?

They will if you skip entire pages. They think they paid to hear something that you have omitted. My audiences want so much of my brain that they call it to my attention if I miss even one line in the outline. However, remember that my outline is much sketchier than yours so each line is a major thought.

" " Quotes On Speaking

Great speakers listen to the audience
with their eyes.

Anonymous

He rose without a friend
and sat down without an enemy.

Henry Gratton

If the stories you're telling have been told by others, or
can be told by someone else, get rid of it. I did that
years ago and my speech has become completely
original. It's the law of supply and demand that has
grown my business.

Art Berg CSP, CPAE

Marketing

Marketing is your lifeblood in this business. Without marketing, you will be the greatest speaker the world will never know. You must let people know who you are, and what you have to offer. This is the longest chapter in the book, because, well...it needs to be! Almost every newer speaker is shocked to discover how much time they need to put in on marketing every day, and every week. It's an ongoing activity in this business.

First you need to know who your audience is. Then you want to decide if you will position yourself as a speaker or as a consultant who speaks. You want to decide if you'll speak for the meetings industry or the corporate training industry, or both. You will need marketing collateral, such as a website, a press kit, a demo video, and more. At this point you don't need an agent or manager. Most speakers never have these. But many speakers eventually team up with speaker's bureaus, or at least they do speaker showcases. Some fortunate speakers secure lucrative corporate sponsors.

When you begin, you may often speak for free to promote yourself. This is called "speak to market". This gives you exposure, testimonials, referrals and leads for more programs. Regardless of how you market yourself, you MUST become adept at this vital skill.

1. How do I determine who my audience really is?

The audience is the people who need to hear what you have to say. They also determine the content of your programs because it must meet their needs, so it is a bit of a circular problem. You must ask yourself, "Who will pay to hear what I have to say?" Also, "Who needs the information I have to offer?" This requires some research, but is crucial to the success of a professional speaker. Without an audience we are not speakers.

2. How do I know what they want to hear?

Ask them. This can be difficult and inefficient, of course, so you can ask meeting planners who represent associations of people who may want to hear what you have to say. Ask them what keeps their members awake at night. Read industry magazines and see what the hot topics are for their readers. Magazines are great because they only take a few months to publish (rather than years for books) so the information in magazines is much more current.

I read 43 magazines a month to keep abreast of the various industries in which I speak. I don't read every one cover-to-cover, but I scan for hot issues and trends and then read those articles.

3. How do I actually get speaking jobs?

Again, start by speaking for free at service organizations. As you get better, audience members will ask you to speak for their companies. When they start asking, "How much do you charge?" you've got speaking jobs.

4. How do I get leads?

Speaking for free for the right organizations is the key to getting leads. Business speakers can contact the educational directors of Chambers of Commerce or groups like the Elks, Moose, etc. Holistic speakers can contact organizations like the Whole Life Expo and others.

5. What are the benefits of speaking for free for a while?

You will gain experience and potential business. Again, speaking for free in front of the right groups is key. Ask fellow speakers or join organizations like Toastmasters or the National Speakers Association and ask people there where you should speak to hone your skills and find paid engagements.

6. Should I be a generalist or a specialist?

There's too much competition in being a generalist, or a pure motivational speaker, or on such topics as teamwork, change or sales. Specialize in an area that you can make your own. While there may be fewer speaking opportunities, it's much easier and less expensive to market a specialty topic than a general one.

7. Is it best to position myself as a speaker who consults, or as a consultant who speaks?

It really depends on your expertise. If you are already a consultant, then be a consultant first and market yourself as a speaker second. If you are primarily a speaker, then use your speaking engagements to look for consulting opportunities. For instance, at the end of every speech I remind the audience that I'm available for more in-depth consulting.

I have obtained several lucrative consulting jobs as a result of my speaking on diversity. I then come back and work with managers and CEO's to help reduce the potential for sexual harassment and racial discrimination complaints.

8. How important is it to establish myself as an expert in my topic?

If you're not an expert why should anyone hire you to help them? Again, it's difficult to be an expert at everything (generalist) but it's rather easy to be an expert in some specific area (specialist). One hour of intensive study a day will give you the equivalent of more than six full-semester college courses a year.

9. Do I need to have a publicist or advertising agency help me?

If you have a very time-sensitive topic or hot book, a publicist or advertising agency can be of tremendous help in getting publicity for you. Most beginning speakers can barely afford the stamps to send press releases much less an expensive professional to assist them. Fortunately, there are very inexpensive community colleges who offer courses in advertising and marketing.

10. Do agents book speakers?

Agents generally represent high-profile speakers and other famous people. They do not usually actively seek work for their clients but rather□coordinate their appearances for a fee ranging from 15 to 25 percent of the appearance fee. Most bureaus are not interested in speakers unless they are consistently earning at least $1,500 per speech. There's a sad but true saying that, "Speakers bureaus don't need you until you don't need them". If you're well-known enough to attract the attention of a bureau, you probably have plenty of business already.

11. How do I get a corporate sponsor?

You must have a product or subject that would logically link to a sponsor. Ask yourself , "What kind of company would benefit from associating with me?" For instance, if you're known for speaking about your mountain climbing experiences, you might get a parka company to sponsor you. Obviously, corporate sponsors are difficult for speakers to obtain. Try looking at who sponsors speakers whose topics are similar to yours and contact their competitors.

12. Are there companies that would underwrite my book?

Few companies underwrite books unless there is a direct benefit to them. Again, you must ask, "Who would benefit from associating themselves with my book?" Even if you find a sponsor, you must ask yourself how much of the profits will you give-up in exchange for upfront money?

13. What various forms of marketing collateral should I have?

If you specialize you really don't need very much marketing material. A description of the programs you present might be sufficient. If you are a generalist, you will be competing with people who have fancy four-color slick brochures. Try to videotape every program you present, whether for pay or for free. If you have unique content that people want to hear, they don't need to be sold with a lot of fancy marketing materials.

14. How important is one's reputation in this business?

We are in a service and entertainment business and your reputation is crucial to your success. If people believe and trust you they will buy your products and recommend you to others. If they think you lack integrity they won't dare risk their own reputations by referring you. A reputation takes years to develop and only seconds to destroy.

15. I have heard that the speaking world is a small one, that bureaus all know one another, and that meeting planners talk among themselves?

What can I say? Yes, it's a very tightly-knit community composed of people who love to share information. If, for example, you cut your fee for one, you might as well plan to discount it for everyone. Many former speakers wonder why they can't get work simply because they treated one client carelessly.

16. Should I have a general one-sheet, with all my programs and topics listed?

Yes, it's a good way to give potential clients and bureaus a sense of your topic areas. Don't list too many divergent topics. Specialize, specialize, specialize.

17. What is a press kit and what should be in it?

It varies. At a minimum a press kit contains the one-sheet, your biography, a few testimonial letters and a demo videotape. If you have written a book that should be included as well. The press kit should be customized to the media outlet or bureau that is requesting it. That's the beauty of a computer and color printer these days. You don't have to store dozens of different one-sheets or brochures.

18. Should I have individual one-sheets on every program I offer?

You don't need different one-sheets. However, you should have a one-page detailed description of your major topics. Put these on your website as separate pages so clients can download them.

19. Should I include testimonials in my press kit and marketing materials?

It's nice to use some quotes and testimonial letters. They add some credibility but rarely make a huge difference in the decision to hire a speaker. Either they like you and your topic or they don't. However, remember that they must buy you first, then your unique topic.

20. Can a speaker use a national brand company name on their client list if they speak at a local branch of it?

This is a question of ethics. Unless you addressed the whole company it's more honest to list the name of the company followed by the specific branch or division that hired you. If you specialize that's crucial because speaking to a broad audience might actually hurt your credibility rather than help it. For instance, I presented a program on diversity to the United States Department of Agriculture--Equal Opportunity Division. Doesn't it make more sense to list it that way than simply the "USDA"? Why on earth would they be interested in a diversity seminar? In other words, to not be specific actually raises more questions than proving credibility.

21. How does a speaker break into the major leagues?

Just like ballplayers, to break into the majors you must hone your craft in the minors. This means giving a minimum of fifty presentations for little or no money to civic or business groups. During this time you will refine your presentation, improve your delivery and find a unique niche. As you progress you will slowly raise your fees until you find yourself in the majors. Unless you have a hit book or your subject just suddenly resonates with a national audience, it will take time and a lot of work.

By regularly attending meetings of groups like Toastmasters or the National Speakers Association you will learn how to take your speaking to the next level. Along the way you must master marketing, topic development, platform skills and other competencies.

Unfortunately, becoming a successful professional speaker is not a linear, predictable career path. There have been many times in my career that I felt I was stuck and would never be able to move forward until I met someone in a similar position or listened to an audio tape that helped me break through to the next level. Professional speaking takes perseverance, hard work and a bit of luck.

22. What are the various markets that hire speakers?

You'd be surprised what markets hire speakers. In addition to major companies and associations, churches, social groups, civic organizations, and schools all hire professional speakers, trainers and facilitators. Every type of business could use the services of a professional speaker, but some are more willing to pay than others.

Remember that it's harder for speakers to develop credibility in some markets than others. For instance, the medical and legal fields prefer to have peers speak to them as opposed to laypersons.

23. When I speak for free, how do I decide who my strategic groups would be?

When you speak for free you must have a clear goal in mind because there is an endless array of groups who would be happy to have you perform your services for nothing. There are three main reasons professional speakers give free presentations: 1) to let an organization sample their skills and program content; 2) to get in front of potential clients; and 3) to support an organization they feel strongly about.

When giving a sample speech or presentation, be sure not to give them so much they feel that they don't need more of your services. A sample program should be just that--a sample. Every program you present, especially those for free, should leave the audience wanting more.

When providing a program to potential decision makers, give highlights of your best material. It never hurts to apologize, saying: "I'm sorry we don't have more time because I'd love to share my secrets for getting business while playing golf or skiing." or "The next time book me for twice as long so I can tell you how to get people to ask you about your product."

When speaking for free at a fund-raiser there's nothing wrong with letting them plug your book or seminars. Make sure your introduction mentions the types of training you provide. Then give one or two main points and reinforce them with solid content and stories.

24. How do I promote my speaking services?

This question could fill a book by itself. Maybe we should write a book entitled, 101 Marketing Tips for Speakers?

Probably the biggest factor that separates successful speakers from those who never seem to make it is marketing. There are thousands of very dynamic presenters each year who fade into oblivion because of lack of visibility. The key is to become well-known in the market you know best and then to expand out from there.

In a nutshell, here are the basic steps to promoting a speaker:

- Focus on an audience you want to speak to.

- Determine who the decision-makers are for that audience.

- Analyze what are the most effective means of reaching those decision-makers.

- Develop a marketing plan that hits decision-makers on a quarterly basis because you never know when they will be hiring.

- Follow-up after every presentation to get letters of recommendation. Add planners who hire you to your database so they are reminded every quarter about your services.

- Write a book on the subject you know best. A book is often the best marketing tool for speakers.

- Expand into other related or similar industries. You never want to have all of your speaking engagements in only one industry in case of an economic downturn in that sector.

Some of the more common ways speakers promote themselves include:

- Direct mail to meeting planners

- Ads in magazines that reach meeting planners

- Cold calls to meeting planners

- Giving notepads to attendees with the speaker's contact information on them

- Ads in telephone Yellow Pages

- Websites

25. What is the most effective way to market yourself as a speaker?

Word-of-mouth recommendations from planners and attendees at your presentations.

26. How can you be sure a magazine or other ad is worth it before you place it?

Contact other speakers who are advertising in the same media and ask them about their results.

27. How can I do low-budget promotion?

The best promotion is word-of-mouth from planners and attendees at your presentations. They know how good you are and can sell you with enthusiasm. Make sure they know how to refer you to others by giving them notepads, pens and other items with your name and contact information on it.

Get the name and e-mail address of every attendee and then send them an e-mail newsletter either monthly or quarterly. Develop a newsletter of value to people who hire you. As a speaker you are in a perfect position to see what issues are becoming hot in their industry, so take some time to become knowledgeable and write about it.

Write articles for magazine in the industry you want to reach. This positions you as an expert and gives you constant visibility if you write a continuing column.

28. What are speaker's showcases and should I do them?

Showcases are where speakers can present a sample of their programs in front of planners. The quality of a showcase depends on the kinds of people who attend. If people who hire speakers like yourself are in the audience it can be very worthwhile. If no one shows up it's a waste of time.

To make a showcase worth your time, be sure that the program will be professionally videotaped. This way, even if you do not get any bookings you will at least get some new footage you can add to your promotional video. You should also look at the list of people the showcase promoter is inviting to the program. If these are not the kind of people who would hire you as a speaker, don't do the showcase. Just because planners are invited and attend, they may not be the right people to hire you.

Remember that a showcase is just that-a sample of your best work. Demonstrate your best presentation skills, then show a variety of the topics you cover. Give as many "ahas" (unique ideas) as possible.

Also, ask the promoter what their experience is with producing successful showcases. You might even ask to see a list of planners who actually attended their last showcase. Again, if these are not the kind of people who would hire you it's a waste of your time.

29. What is a speaker's bureau?

Speakers bureaus are organizations that book speakers at companies and events. Bureaus do not market speakers. In other words, they do not promote any particular speaker but rather spend their time marketing to planners. When they find a planner who is looking for a speaker the bureau then matches the planners requirements with several potential speakers. These requirements might include: subject matter, budget, location, experience, and more.

I own a speakers bureau, and we have 3,000 speakers in a computer database. When we find a planner who has a need we then sort the speakers by subject and budget first. Then we look at the list and the planner's other requirements and suggest several potential speakers. Most planners want to see a demo video of the speakers and maybe also talk to the speaker.

Bureaus get paid a 20 percent-30 percent commission based on the gross speaking fee paid to the speaker. Reputable bureaus do not charge a registration fee because they should only get paid if they perform. Some bureaus charge fees for viewing videotapes and giving written critiques or other services and I think this is acceptable since they are performing a service for their fee.

A speaker should present a clear image to a bureau. In other words, don't tell a bureau that you can speak on any topic they need. No one is an expert at everything and how can a bureau remember a speaker who does not have a niche? Develop a niche and stick to it. This way your books and videos will all be consistent with that specialty. Also, the bureau will be able to associate you with a particular niche.

It's sad but true that bureaus don't need you until you need them. Most bureaus are not interested in a speaker until they are earning a consistent $1,500-2,000 minimum for a keynote. Think about it-a 20 percent commission on a $500 fee is only $100, whereas the same commission on a $2,000 fee is $400. That's four-times the amount of income for the same booking.

When you are consistently commanding $1,500 or more for a keynote, contact bureaus who book speakers in your subject category. Dottie Walters publishes a book of bureaus throughout the country.

When a bureau agrees to accept your materials, send them a bureau-friendly one sheet and video. Bureau-friendly materials do not include the speaker's contact information. This means no physical address, no phone number, no e-mail address and no Website. Even referring to your city in your bio can be considered unfriendly by bureaus. For instance, innocently referring to the fact that you teach at the University of California at Berkeley enables clients to contact you directly through the school instead of going through the bureau. Bureaus spend a lot of money and time booking speakers. Make sure they get paid for their efforts.

If you want to really get booked by bureaus become pro-bureau. This means taking the time to print the bureaus contact information on your materials. This saves them a lot of time and says you really want to work with the bureau. You can be involved with only one bureau, or have relationships with many bureaus all across the country and world.

Don't forget that bureaus have incredibly high expenses in staffing, overhead and marketing. They have no guarantee of receiving any income regardless of the amount of money they spend. It's a difficult business, which the Internet is making ever harder. Now that many speakers have their own websites many planners are searching the Internet directly instead of going through bureaus. We bureaus must find a way to add value and save planners time if we are going to survive as a profession.

30. How do I get more engagements from a speech I give?

Try to make every presentation better than the last. Subtly remind people at the end that you are available for other programs. Make sure every planner gives you a letter of recommendation. Have them refer you to other divisions in their company or organization.

31. How can I get free videos of me speaking?

Any time you speak put in your contract that the organizer is to videotape your speaking. You may have to reduce your fee to pay for the added expense but it's worth it. If you can't get a video at least record the audio. This way you might be able to turn the program into an audiocassette album. At the worst you will be able to critique your speaking style and content with the audio tape.

Sometimes when you speak for free you can at least have them videotape you. You may have to provide your own camera, lights and microphone, but have them assign someone to operate the camera.

Contact a local community college or university video department. They often have students who would like the experience of videotaping a speaker. You may have to pay $50-100 to get their help but again it's worth it.

32. How important is it to have a demo video?

If you are recommended by a planner or past attendee you probably don't need one. However, when speaking to a group or company for the first time you will almost always need a demo video. Also, bureaus require them because it's a standard part of the decision-making process by planners.

Demo videos are usually around 15-minutes long with segments of your best material on it. After that you may want to add a full-length keynote. However, most planners decide to book speakers after the first three or four minutes so start with your best material.

If you speak on different subjects you will want to have different videos for each. Label each clearly so you don't get them mixed-up.

If you are going to produce a demo video make it a professional one. Use television lighting, a high-quality camera and a wireless microphone. Do not record on VHS format video since it degrades badly when editing. You wouldn't believe the demo videos I have received where you can hardly see the unlit speaker in a dark room or hardly hear them from the microphone on the camera thirty feet away or both. Demo videos can cost from $500 for a basic-level version to many thousands of dollars for the very best.

33. How important is it to have a demo audio tape?

More planners probably listen to audio tape demos than watch videos. These are easy to record and duplicate. This is another good reason to audio tape every program you present.

34. When people contact your speaker's bureau, do they do so by topic? (I've been told to make sure you sell yourself by topic, due to this), Or do they ask for speakers by name, if well known? Both?

Mostly by topic. For instance, yesterday someone asked about "Media Training" and another about "Motivation". We divide out speakers by subject, location and fee range. The computer system will cull by any parameter we want. This is why you want a unique topic.

35. Do Silicon Valley companies work through speaker's bureaus, or do bureaus mainly see associations and special events, rather than training requests?

It's about 50/50. I get calls from Oracle and HP all the time.

36. I've been told that one should have a "bureau-friendly" website, with no contact information other than to a bureau. Is this a trend?

I really don't know. Most planners still don't look to the web first before calling a bureau. However, if they go to the web they will not only get your bureau-friendly site but you bureau-unfriendly site as well. What's the point? I just prepare bureau-friendly materials for bureaus that hire me.

37. I've also been told that one should have a section in one's website aimed

at meeting planners, who buy speakers, and a separate one aimed at corporations, who buy trainers. Do you find this to be a trend also?

I don't know about whether it's a trend or not. My website has a special section for planners. It gets a lot of action and will do even better once I add a couple of links.

38. In general, which market is it harder to crack for newer speakers, the meetings industry or the corporate training industry?

If you have a corporate background this is probably an easier place to start. It's a much more targeted market. The meetings industry is still composed of individual companies in specific markets. They are harder to find. Associations are a very tough nut to crack. Again, if you are well-known in the industry it will be easier.

39. Is the answer different for established speakers?

An established speaker going into a new industry is just as unknown as anyone else. If they have a book on the subject it helps and so does their marketing savvy but that's about all.

40. In your experience, when people ask about your services, how do you respond? Do you respond in like manner to them? If they email, do you email back, even though they provide full contact information? Or is it better to call, since the request is a hot one, and you don't want it to cool off?

I usually respond in the same manner as they contact me unless they seem particularly interested and give me other contact information. I can e-mail flyers, video, etc. However, a lot of people are not tech-savvy so I will fax and then e-mail as a back-up.

41. What percentage increase would you suggest for a client not having the three referrals to me on time?

I usually threaten them with a $500 fee increase. I've never had to charge it, though. There's nothing wrong with requesting, in writing, referrals if they like your program. It's one of the things I use when people can't afford my full fee. I require a letter and three referrals. I usually do this anyway but I don't tell them that.

42. Do you keep or remove the dates on testimonial letters so they become timeless and can be used forever? Or should we rotate the new in and remove the old?

I keep the dates on to show people how long I have been presenting a particular program.

43. In my marketing collateral, should I mainly stress what benefits they get from hearing me?

FOCUS! From the first word to the last, nothing should be sent that doesn't relate to the subject at hand. You have very little time to grab their interest.

Have you ever heard of the advertising motto AIDA?

ATTENTION: You must grab the audience's attention first, otherwise all the rest is wasted. This is the headline or title.

INTEREST: Once you have their attention you must immediately generate interest in your program. These are the promises.

DESIRE: Once you have their interest you must make them want you to deliver on your promises. These are the benefits.

ACTION: Once you've got them drooling over the benefits (what's in it for ME) you make the call to action. "Call now" or "operators are standing by" and give them an 800 number.

44. You suggest that if I get a gig with a corporation or small business, then I should tap them for more work. Do you suggest taking work with them that is out of my "passion area"? i.e. that is not my flagship, or hottest program? Should I be taking work with them that I don't do (e.g., if they want time management, which is not in my offerings), but could whip up a program fast, to improve cash flow and build a stronger relationship with them?

First, talk to corporations about what their "passion area" is. Then you can:

1. Adjust your program to meet their need.

2. Develop a new program for them for which you could develop passion.

3. Refer the program on to a bureau or another speaker.

You must know what the companies you are working for need. What keeps them awake at night?

Recognize that you won't always be doing your main program. For example, I often develop a relationship with companies through my Multicultural Programs, but the next year their people have heard the material and they like me but want something new. I deliver a program on time management, stress management, etc. that is more motivational.

45. How do you actively seek referrals and what do you suggest? Clint Maun, CSP, says he makes part of his pay three or four actual referrals from people who can hire him, in addition to the actual money. He has it in his contract and says so right up front. Is this something you see as viable?

There's nothing wrong with requesting, in writing, referrals if they like your program. It's one of the things I use when people can't afford my full fee. I require a letter and three referrals. To get your referrals add this to your contract, "Fee to be $. In the event a minimum of three referrals are not received by... then fee to be $".

46. How do you stay in touch with past clients? Do you make calls, and if so, what do you say to them? Do you use written materials, and if so what do you send? Do you email, and if so what do you include? Do you give gifts, and if so, what do you give? How often do they hear from you on a regular basis?

Put your past clients into a database and send them a newsletter periodically. Give them generic marketing tips and information about you. Try to stay in touch at least three times a year. If I send any gift it must be useable on their desk. I've send post-it note pads with my name and phone, pens, etc.

47. Do you find that the sales cycle in corporations is longer than for associations or smaller businesses?

Associations are the longest because of the bureaucracy and financial constraints. Corporations are next. Smaller businesses are the fastest because the communications link to decision-makers is shorter.

48. Do I actually ask them what their passion area is? How do I phrase this? In person? By phone? In a survey?

It's best to take the personal approach. Ask them in person or on the phone: "What issues keep you awake at night"? This makes you sound like a deep-thinking consultant. Then you can:

1. Adjust your program to meet their need.

2. Develop a new program for them for which you could develop passion.

3. Refer the program on to a bureau or another speaker.

49. Do you agree with the often-heard phrase, "We are in the marketing business first, the expert speaker business next and the speaking business last."? (We are marketers and sellers and lastly speakers). What percent of time should starting speakers spend on marketing and sales efforts?

I heartily agree. This is why most aspiring speakers are not successful despite being talented on the platform. Fortunately, I have a marketing background and the need for marketing is obvious to me. Most speakers would be really surprised how important marketing really is. I probably spend 70 percent of my time marketing and 30 percent speaking. This would include writing articles for magazines, giving interviews, writing books, sending out letters and press kits, developing marketing materials, working on my website, etc.

50. How can I tell if this might be a big client, one that would help position me further?

You never really know who's going to turn into a big client. I did a program for the National Association of Music Merchants in 1996 after chasing them for two years. I expect to do a dozen full-fee programs for them this year. Oracle, on the other hand, has never called me back in.

" " Quotes On Speaking

If you have an important point to make, don't try to be subtle or clever. Use the pile driver. Hit the point once. Then come back and hit it again. Then hit it a third time; a tremendous whack.

Winston Churchill

It is delivery that makes the orators success.

Johann Wolfgang Von Goethe

Develop personal stories. Personal stories are self-revealing that bond speaker and listener. Your stories will grow and soon become signature stories that can be used as metaphors and adapted to every audience.

Grady Jim Robinson, CSP, CPAE

Developing Products

Many newer professional speakers are quite surprised to learn that they can earn as much, or even more from product sales, as they can from speaking fees. Products give you credibility and passive income. As we say in this industry, "Make it once, and sell it many times". With product you leverage your time and productivity immensely.

Make it a habit to audiotape and videotape all your talks and turn them into products. You can also use these recordings as feedback about your performances. You want to learn how to make, market and sell BOR (Back of room) products. Consider writing and producing a book, which you can sell and use as a business card and also as a negotiating tool. Surprisingly, you can often charge more for a well-done special report on a narrow topic your audiences find valuable. Take a deep dive into product creation. You'll find it fascinating, fun and quite pleasing to your pocketbook.

1. How often should I audiotape my programs?

Speech coaches will tell you to audiotape every program you present. First, you will quickly learn to improve your speaking by eliminating "filler words" such as "er" or "uh" and you'll find ways to get better as a speaker by comparing your speeches to others. Second, you never know when you will come up with a great program that could be sold as part of, or as a complete product. This is one of the best ways for new speakers to develop product.

Audiotapes are inexpensive to produce and they're still the most popular product sold by speakers.

2. How can I use audiotapes as marketing tools, in addition to using them as product?

You can send all or a portion of an audiotape to people who are likely to hire you, such as bureaus or planners. They are much more likely to find the time to evaluate a tape while driving to work in the car than sitting down and watching a video demo at home or in the office. You may also want to give them away at your seminars as prizes or gifts. You never know when they'll wind-up in the hands of someone who may be able to hire you. Remember, you've got to market, market, market.

3. What types of handouts do audiences expect? Workbooks? Handouts? Checklists? High Content?

It depends on the type of audience and the venue. At keynote speeches that generally last an hour to 90-minutes, most attendees don't expect an outline. Most high-energy keynoters don't want their audiences distracted by having to follow an outline. However, giving them a business-card-sized checklist of the main points with your contact information is a great way to give them extra value and make them remember you.

Speakers that provide seminars that run from 90-minutes to 3-hours usually give a brief handout that covers the main points of their program. There is usually plenty of "white space" between the points for participants to make notes. Put your biography and contact data on the handouts so people can reach you for more information.

Workshops that run 3-hours to 6-hours or longer generally include a workbook. People who attend programs of this length expect that their time has been spent wisely in a high-content workshop and sometimes the thickness of the workbook is an indication of the value in their minds. You may want to put references and other collateral materials in the back of your workbook.

The cost of a program can dictate the quality and amount of material that attendees are provided. In a very expensive program attendees may receive audio or videotapes in addition to a very extensive workbook.

4. What are the costs of producing a book, versus an audiotape?

Amazingly, the cost of printing a book and copying are very similar. A one-hour audiotape costs about a dollar to produce while a small paperback book can cost a dollar or two to print. However, when you package six audiotapes together into an album you can charge $59 to $99 for a total cost of less than $10. Knowing how to package your products is key to getting maximum value.

5. How do I sell books at quantity discounts prior to a program?

You can sell them to planners for what bookstores might sell them for. Knocking about a third off your retail price is a good place to start. If your book retails for $29.95 you might offer it to them for $19.95. You need to sell any product for about three-times your costs to make money.

Don't forget to offer your products to attendees at a discount if they buy in quantity. Package your products together to add value and increase your profit margin. I sell many more of the booklets I offer by selling them for $70 for four instead of $19.95 each. While it's only a $10 discount on an $80 purchase, people love a bargain!

6. Is it true experienced speakers lament that they wished they had developed product sooner in their career?

Absolutely, I have a six-cassette album on negotiating, a five-cassette album on Coaching Generation-X Employees, four special reports that earn me more than my speaking fee and an interactive CD-ROM just being finished. Product gives you credibility and passive income. Attend every NSA program you can on developing product.

7. What is back of the room sales (BOR)?

BOR sales are sales of your products during breaks and after a program. I often sell three-times the amount of my fee in product. The key to successful back of the room sales is to be subtle and make it an integral part of the program. If you have a book, refer to it. If you have tapes, tell the audience how the tapes can help them. In other words, sprinkle your promotions throughout your program rather than in one concentrated sales pitch.

I sell a list of 100 things real estate agents do for their clients. My most effective promotion is saying, "You don't need my list because you can make your own." On the other hand, just think how much time it would take you to come up with 100 activities. Makes $19.95 seem rather insignificant, doesn't it?

Remember that your materials will be around long after you have finished the program. You are doing your attendees a tremendous service by giving them a little of you to take home.

8. What are some of the best BOR products for newer speakers to create and sell?

Whatever you have that your attendees will pay for are good BOR products. I never thought to sell my list of 100 things agents do for their clients until I mentioned it and a couple of people asked if they could buy it.

Start with a list or small report. A report of 40-50 pages can be sold for $19.95 and only costs about $2.00 to print. This is a much higher profit margin than selling a book you have written through a major publishing house which usually only pay authors $2-$3 per book sold.

Record your programs and sell audio or videotapes. Make them into interactive CD-ROMs. You would not believe the kind of stuff that attendees buy from speakers. Here is a list of things I am aware of that speakers regularly sell:

- Bookmarks
- Note pads with the speaker's contact information on it
- Dolls that look like the speaker
- Posters of the speaker
- Key chains
- Kush balls
- Booklets
- Special reports
- Lists
- CD-ROMs

9. What is your view on the strategies behind doing a book in hardcover vs. in soft cover?

I would go with hard cover if it's your primary book and talk. It's not that much more expensive but the difference in credibility is amazing.

10. I am told that mass duplicating of less-than studio-quality original tapes results in poorer and poorer quality. I've also heard that people don't mind "live" audios and that studio-quality DAT tapes (Digital Audio Tapes) are not necessary, as long as the audio book jacket makes you look like a pro.

Yes, quality is not paramount, and personally I like the audience interaction.

11. I'm also told that many people buy books and tapes and never open them up. They just want a piece of you after they hear you.

This is true. Once, there was a problem with one of my tapes in a six-cassette album and I got calls years later for people who just discovered the problem.

12. Do you find that people share your books with others? What's an example?

I got a nice letter from a woman who intercepted one of my books sent to a real estate association and liked it so much she highlighted it. Now she wants another clean copy to send to the association. She happens to be in charge of the convention for next year and now wants to book me. This would never happen with a tape.

13. What system do you use to write books and articles?

I use "Dragon Naturally Speaking" to dictate my thoughts and then reorganize them using Word.

14. How do you budget time to write per project? Or do you just keep going until you finish?

For a book I try to write five pages per day. That's 35 pages a week; which is a chapter. In 12 weeks I have a book. Discipline is the key to success in anything.

15. How do you leverage content for various products? (Compared to starting over and re-inventing the wheel)

I start writing articles first and then use them as the basis for various chapters in my books. I save each one on a separate disk for each book title.

Audios come from my seminars. I simply record them using a high-quality microphone and DAT recorder. I then have them digitally edited.

16. What system do you have for producing class notes for your seminars?

I begin by putting ideas for a seminar randomly in word processing. Then I try to organize them into logical groups. Finally, I organize the flow-introductory material first, then build to the next level and finally the conclusion.

The key is, "What do I want people to know when they leave?" That guides development and content. Remember, if they can leave with one useful idea they will feel the program was valuable.

17. How do you market and sell your special reports?

You won't believe it. Most average about 40 pages, unbound and single-sided. Because of the unique content I will sell 20-30 to a group of 25 for $19.95 each.

18. You said that speakers of your level can make 50% to 100% to 150% of the speaking fee by selling product. This fascinates me, the passive end. Do CSPmlevel folks, who have product, typically run these percentages?

Most that have product do. Some people are an exception. They have no books or tapes. They'd make a lot more money if they did. At every program I always talk to the audience and ask, "What issues keep you awake at night?" That led to my second most popular program, "Runnin' with the Big Dogs" on how to compete with larger competitors.

Product gives you credibility and passive income. Attend every NSA program you can on developing product.

19. I have heard people will buy audios even if they are "basic" looking and sounding. What is your experience?

If it is a niche market like real estate they are a lot more forgiving than the general public. I make color copy covers and slip them into the cassettes.

20. Do you have any tips for writing fast, while still being able to maintain high quality?

Write every day. Don't worry about quality until you go back to edit. If you worry about quality initially you will never write. If I knew the answer to this I'd be rich! My trick is to write a lot and then boil it down to just the stuff that blows people away.

I start every seminar by giving people something they didn't know before. This gets their attention and gives me credibility from the start. After that, almost everything I say seems to be accepted better.

21. Your book you showed me had the look and feel of a "real book" from a trade house, although I remember you told me later you self-published. It's a great-looking book, and I'm sure it opens many doors.

If you are going to self-publish it's got to look good. I've seen self-published books that were printed crooked with tons of typos. Again, today you can print as few as 100 books at a time. My next book is going to be done that way, called print-on-demand.

22. What is your typical system for using books as a business tool? Is it anything like the Bob Burg system of mailing it to top execs and decision makers, with follow-up?

Mine are too expensive to do that. His are paperback. Right now I am sending free copies to all of the Directors of Education for Coldwell Banker across the country. There are less than 20 but what do you think the chances are they will recommend it to their agents? I will also send a press kit to every state Association of Realtors in the country and write an article for their magazines.

23. Do you do book pre-sales at quantity discount at your programs?

Yes, I sold nearly 100 of my current book and we have over 100 orders for the book due out in February. We offered a pre-sale discount from $34.95 to $29.95 and promised it autographed. It basically paid for the printing costs.

24. How do I set up an audio system to tape my talks?

The problem with some people's audio setup is that they have to change the tape every 45 minutes or so. If you miss one tape change you miss the entire day.

My setup is remote so someone else can change the tapes without interrupting the program. I can load it with two-hour tapes so they only need to be changed hourly.

For a really important program I connect my gear to an S-VHS camera which will record up to two-hours on a hi-fi channel without needing a change. I plan for my break at the 1:45 mark so we can change tapes during a three-hour program.

25. When you speak, do you have a catalogue of all your products you distribute?

I have a brochure for my real estate products and flyers for my others.

26. Do you bring all your products for BOR, if appropriate?

Only those I think I will sell at a specific venue. I hate to send product if I can help it.

27. Have you ever hired anyone to write for you? I've heard some speakers hire college kids or teachers for this. Do you know many speakers who do this?

I've never hired anyone to do this but am considering it. The problem is by the time I have drafted the outline for them I've pretty much written the program.

28. Where do you write? On the road, at home, etc.?

Yes. All of the above. I bring my laptop and do most of my writing on airplanes or in airports. Last year I spent some 200+ hours there so I got a lot of work done!

29. What are the various price points I should have for my products?

Charge whatever you can get. Remember, if you products are unique they can't get them anywhere else and have to pay what you charge if they want it.

Always offer a discount for quantity purchases. I have four reports for $19.95 each but I sell all four for only $70. I know I sell a lot more of the less popular reports as a bundle then separately.

30. I write most of my workbooks and audience handouts in a fill-in-the-page format. People seem to like it and are OK (we fill them in as we go) that I don't have tons of text. I also provide articles I've written, that have the text they want. Is it OK using the workbook style or do people expect lots of checklists, tables, charts, etc.?

It depends on the program. If I were doing a series of day-long programs for an in-house group I would add more detail that could be used throughout the program. For a three-hour class you want to balance between making them write notes and having them pay attention. I wouldn't stress the pages so much but rather use section numbers. This would have cut at least a third of the pages out of your workbook with no loss in content. If you focus on what you want your audience to leave with you will have much more forceful headings.

31. Do you suggest larger point size in the workbook? I use 12 point and a friend suggested using 14 or 16 point, which is helpful for audiences with older eyes.

For most groups I put the headings in 14-point and the rest in 12-point. For older groups I would go up to 16/14.

32. How do you time your seminar to the length of the workbook? Do you have a standard workbook for each program, and then just clip it or lengthen it for a 1/2 day, full day, 2-day, 3-day seminar? Or do you keep the workbook and just skip portions of it and tell them it is bonus material?

There really is no rule-of-thumb for timing a workbook. It really depends on the amount of material you are trying to cover, technical vs. non-technical information, and audience interaction.

Be careful about putting too much information in a workbook. Sometimes people think you just ran out of time and feel cheated in the content of your program. Also, you may be able to sell some of that other material as a separate "report".

Quotes On Speaking

It's not so much knowing when to speak,
but when to pause.

Jack Benny

Only the prepared speaker
deserves to be confident.

Dale Carnegie

Since the best speakers in the world are originals, you
might as well start out that way. Develop your materials
first, and then go watch other "experts". Start out
respecting your own originality, and you'll never regret
it.

Janelle Barlow, Ph.D., CSP

Setting Fees

Setting your fee structure correctly is as much an art as it is a science. To do this, you'll want to research your competitor's fee structure. It's important to know how and when to transition from free speaking into part-time professional speaking, and then into full-time professional speaking. You might be able to position yourself as a consultant, as well as a speaker. That can be very lucrative and efficient. You may want to charge different prices for different types of audiences, such as non-profits vs. corporations. You will want to learn how to negotiate your fees, when to raise your fees, and what the fee levels are for a beginning pro speaker, a journeyman pro and an established pro speaker. Setting the correct prices on your services is very important. Think this through carefully. Do your due diligence and talk to other speakers in your topic area and at your level of speaking.

1. How do I know when to quit my day job and begin speaking full-time?

Easy. When you can live on your speaking income it's time to make the move. Most speakers, however, probably kept working part-time at a "real job" until they felt comfortable enough to make the transition to full-time speaking. Don't worry, you'll know when it's time.

2. How does a speaker break into the major leagues?

It depends on what you consider the "Major Leagues". Perhaps what you mean is the top level of speakers who regularly earn $5,000 and more per program. The fastest way is to have a mega best-selling book. Short of that you just keep working to become better with every speech or seminar and keep raising your fees. Eventually you'll reach a point that you are happy with in terms of numbers of dates per year and fee per program.

3. How can I combine consulting with speaking?

Towards the end of every program you can mention your consulting services and how it might benefit your audience. Consulting generally pays less per hour than speaking but is more steady. Also, you can schedule consulting around your speaking engagements to smooth out the "peaks and valleys" of irregular speaking income.

4. Is the cash flow better for consulting than speaking?

Cash flow in consulting is generally steadier but not necessarily more lucrative than speaking. I'm fortunate that my consulting on sexual harassment and racial discrimination prevention pays nearly the same as my speaking fee. I understand that's rather unusual in the consulting business so don't expect it.

5. Are the per diems lower for consulting than for speaking?

Per diems can be higher for consulting since you will spend a longer time on-site and away from home. You want your per diem payment to cover your living expenses so you don't lose money due to food, local travel costs and other expenses.

6. Should I have discounts in my fees for various groups, such as non-profits?

You may decide to offer a discount for non-profits but I'm not sure why. If your service is worth a certain amount it should be worth even more to those who need it more such as non-profit organization. Remember, non-profits have budgets for speakers, but they're just not taxed on net income. I help a certain number of non-profit groups every year by offering to do a keynote speech as a fundraiser.

7. Is it standard to charge the audience or meeting planner for my handouts?

No, it's rather rare to charge for handouts unless it goes beyond the usual. If you include a binder with reference material you might be able to tack on an extra fee for it. However, most planners will copy handouts from a master you provide so there is no cost to you. I give out an order form for my products separately since many planners will eliminate any such material when they are making copies to save money.

8. Can you use book or other product sales as a fee negotiation strategy?

Certainly. You can offer to include a free book for every attendee if they pay your full fee. If a book costs you $3 each it can be a cost-effective way to maintain your fee integrity. Or you can offer to give your book to every attendee for only $5 if they pay your full fee. This way you not only encourage them to pay you what you're worth but also net $2 a book! The strategies are only limited by your imagination.

9. Why do even established speakers continue to speak for free sometimes?

Probably the most common reason is to raise funds for causes we feel strongly about. Instead of donating a hundred dollars to a non-profit organization we will often speak for free to raise thousands of dollars for the same group. This is using our talents to do good.

The other reason established speakers sometimes speak for free is to get in front of people who could book them in the future. The Million Dollar Round Table is one such group where anyone in the audience could hire speakers. While it takes time to speak for free, it can save on future marketing efforts.

10. How do I know when to stop speaking 100% for free, and to begin charging?

When you speak on the "animal circuit" (Moose Lodges, Elks Clubs, Lions Clubs, etc.) you will rarely get paid. However, if people come up to you after your presentation and ask you to speak to their companies you should charge them. How much do you charge? I recommend that whatever you think you're worth, double it. Remember, when you quote a fee you can never go up, only down. Even top name speakers may reduce their fees slightly if a program is being held in an attractive destination, such as Hawaii or the Caribbean.

11. Why do you want to double the amount you think you're worth?

Because you never want a meeting planner to say "OK" right away to your fee. If they do, it means you're price is too low. If they hesitate, then you can give them a deal if they will send a letter to attendees for you or agree to buy your book for all participants or something else of equivalent value.

12. What are the benefits of speaking for free for a while?

Again, speaking for free helps you improve your speaking skills, helps refine your topic, and makes contact with potential clients. When speaking for free there is very little risk because the audience's expectations are reduced. It's a little-known fact that many very experienced speakers will do programs for free to test new material. For instance, I spoke for nothing to a group of aspiring speaker because I not only wanted to give back to groups who had helped me along the way but also to try a new close for my program. They got the benefit of my experience and I got to practice the close in front of a very supportive audience. It was a win-win.

13. How do I know when to raise my speaking fees?

When you have more speaking business than you can handle or travel more than you want it's time to raise your fees. As you improve your speaking skills and refine your programs, you are worth more and should probably continually raise your fees. This way you will always have room on your calendar for people who appreciate what you have to offer.

14. How do I know what my speeches and programs are worth?

Your programs are worth what a client will pay. Always quote clients double what you think you are worth. The worse thing that could happen is a client who quickly agrees to your fee. That means you are charging too little.

I have met some very experienced speakers who arrogantly tell me they don't need speakers bureaus because they are fully booked. My response is, your fee is too low. If you're fully booked, raise your fees.

15. What are the normal fee levels for a beginning pro speaker, a journeyman pro and an established pro speaker?

There is no such thing as a normal fee. Beginning speakers charge anywhere from $50 to $500 for keynote. Journeymen speakers may charge $500 to $1,500 for a keynote. Established professional speakers often command $1,500 to $5,000 for a keynote. Well-known professional speakers and minor celebrities get

$5,000 to $12,000. Known celebrities and highly-visible author can earn $12,000 to $25,000. Above that are very unique, highly visible people such as network newscasters, well-known actors, former Presidents, and former military leaders whose fees can approach $100,000 for a keynote.

16. I understand that per diems for consulting are far less than those for speaking. True? But perhaps the cash flow is better with consulting?

Yes, they are less, but they can be more regular, with less travel involved.

17. Do CSP level speakers give discounts on their fees?

CSP speakers (NSA Certified Speaking Professional) will not reduce their fees much. Again, we have so many ways to make it up. I will reduce my fee if they will book me for several programs at a distant location. It saves me travel time and gives me more income than I would have gotten with a full fee. Is that a discount?

18. Is it good to position yourself personally as a consultant? Should I seek to expand speaking jobs into that realm eventually or do I want to remain in "speaking and training"?

The day rate for consulting is about $150-200 an hour but it's a lot steadier and you can also incorporate speaking at full fee. You can also tie it into travel to distant cities. There are a lot of six-figure speakers who do this.

19. Do you charge extra for extra customization?

I don't, unless there is an inordinate amount of customization requested. I think I've only charged extra for customization once or twice.

20. Do you charge a flat fee, a percentage of your fee, an hourly, or a per diem?

It's a flat fee based on how many hours I estimate it will take extra for special customization.

21. Do you do much barter or know other established speakers who do this?

We don't have to barter much. I think most of my clients would consider it somewhat insulting.

🙶 🙷
Quotes On Speaking

It's not how strongly you feel about your topic,
it's how strongly they feel about your topic
after you speak.

Tim Salladay

If you can't write your message in a sentence,
you can't say it in an hour.

Dianna Booher

It is part of our role as professional speakers to be the
champions of the possibilities life has to offer. In fact,
encouraging, inspiring and guiding people along the path
to building a better life are central themes of most
presentations from the platform.

Dr. Peter Legge, LL.D. (Hon), CSP, CPAE, HoF
Author & Professional Speaker

Award-Winning Professional Speakers Share Their Strategies For Going From Free To Fee

In every field of endeavor, it is wise to learn from the best. When you sit at the feet of those who have done what you want to do, you shorten your learning curve dramatically and avoid making mistakes that can hold you back. What better group of experts to consult for moving from free speaking to paid speaking than accomplished professional speakers?

We were very excited to have these high-achieving, award-winning professional speakers offer to send us their strategies for emerging speakers. They well remember what it was like to start out in this business, and they were eager to share their stories, tips and advice for making the transition from free speaker to professional speaker.

Here are the nine speaking gurus who graciously shared their speaking experience with us:

Janelle Barlow, Ph.D., CSP

Art Berg CSP, CPAE

Jeff Blackman, J.D., CSP, CPAE

Patricia Fripp, CSP, CPAE

Roger E. Herman, CSP, CMC

Willie Jolley, CSP, CPAE

Peter Legge, O.B.C., LL.D. (HON.), D.Tech., CSP, CPAE

Lorna Reilly, CSP

Grady Jim Robinson, CSP, CPAE

❝❞ Quotes On Speaking

Our public men are speaking every day on something,
but they ain't saying anything.

Will Rogers

It usually takes me more than three weeks to prepare a
good impromptu speech.

Mark Twain

Be more interested in other folks and their problems,
challenges, hopes and dreams. They are not real
interested in what "you speak on"...unless it will have
some positive impact on their personal or professional
life.

Jeff Blackman, J.D., CSP, CPAE

AWARD WINNING SPEAKER

Janelle Barlow, Ph.D., CSP

Since the best speakers in the world are originals, you might as well start out that way. Whenever I have started to develop new subject areas, people have encouraged me to watch other speakers in that area to see what they were saying and doing in their speeches. I have wisely rejected this advice. Whenever you do this, it becomes tempting to "copy" the approach of others.

Once you start your career this way, it becomes a slippery slope to kissing your originality goodbye. Develop your materials first, and then go watch other "experts." Start out respecting your own originality, and you'll never regret it.

Janelle Barlow, Ph.D., CSP
President TMI, USA
www.tmius.com
Phone: 1 - 702 939 1800
Email: LewisBarlow@tmius.com
8270 West Charleston Boulevard
Las Vegas, NV 89117

Janelle Barlow is president of the multinational training and consulting organization TMI, Inc. She is a licensed marriage and family therapist, and a past board member of the Association of Humanistic Psychology.

Dr. Barlow earned her Ph.D. at the University of California at Berkeley. She also has two master's degrees, one in international relations and another in psychology. Janelle co-wrote a bestselling business book, A Complaint Is a Gift, which is currently available in 20 languages.

She was twice awarded the prestigious "International Trainer of the Year" award by Time Manager International. She also earned the designation of Certified Speaking Professional from the National Speakers Association.

" " Quotes On Speaking

Political speeches are like steer horns. A point here, a point there, and a lot of bull in between.

Alfred E. Neuman

Commencement speeches were invented largely in the belief that outgoing college students should never be released into the world until they have been properly sedated.

G.B. Trudeau

Every night when I go out on stage, there's always one nagging fear in the back of my mind. I'm always afraid that somewhere out there,
there is one person in the audience that
I'm not going to offend!

Don Rickles

From Free to Fee: Becoming a Professional Speaker

AWARD WINNING SPEAKER

Art Berg CSP, CPAE

In 1983, I broke my neck in a serious automobile accident, becoming a quadriplegic. Soon after leaving the hospital, the leader of a local youth group called and asked me to speak to their young men. I gladly agreed, but soon thereafter, other youth groups began to call to make this request. Before long, I was speaking to youth groups, high schools, church groups, and prison inmates all across the country. After seven years, I had spoken for more than 500 times for free.

At one point, I was getting ready to decline any new opportunities to speak. I owned several bookstores at the time and it was becoming increasingly difficult to manage my time with the competing priorities. A friend of mine, aware of my dilemma, convinced me that I should consider speaking for a living. I had never considered this before.

About that same timeframe, a manager from a local company, Novell, called me and asked if I would be willing to speak to his team at an awards banquet. I agreed. He asked me how much I would charge. That was a new question for me. I answered questioningly, "How about fifty bucks?" He laughed. I thought, Oh no,

I am too high! He responded, "I am going to tell my boss you are five hundred dollars so that I don't embarrass you or me." I hung up thinking, Wow, $500 an hour! I was ready to turn pro.

In the summer of 1991, I attended my first convention of the National Speakers Association in Palm Desert, CA. I sat in the back of the room of more than 900 speakers and thought to myself, I can do this. My new career had begun. Since joining NSA, I have done the following:

- Become a CSP (Certified Speaking Professional).

- Been awarded the CPAE Speaker Hall of Fame.

- Travel more than 200,000 miles a year.

- Speak to more than 150,000 people each year.

- Spoke 500 times professionally in the last 3 years.

Have a client list that includes names such as IBM, 3M, HP, Sun Microsystems, Invacare, KeyCorp, Bayer, Sprint, AT&T, NFL's Baltimore Ravens, Pacific Bell, and many other Fortune 500 companies.

While this may sound like an enviable position to be in, let me assure you, it didn't all start out this way. The first few years were hungry ones without much demand for my services. The demand and fees have grown through time somewhat exponentially. Now, I do little (if any) marketing and I still turn down speaking opportunities weekly. As I look back, there were certain things I did which created this wonderful business for me.

I joined the National Speakers Association. Almost everything I learned about being a professional speaker, I learned by actively participating in NSA. I have never missed a National Convention or Winter Workshop since I joined in 1991. I sat in breakout sessions. I took copious notes. I listened to hours of audiotapes. I also joined my local NSA chapter in Utah and actively participated in its leadership and fundraising. You can learn more about NSA at www.nsaspeaker.org It is also a great idea to go to www.speakernetnews.com and join their free email list. They even have a book which has the 1,000 best ideas posted for the last few years. That's one way to make up for lost time.

I spoke 500 times for free. In a seven-year period, I spoke more than 500 times for free to youth groups, church organizations, community groups, and prison inmates. I spoke just for the fun of it. I never intended to do it for a living. If you want to get good, you have to do something a lot. I would suggest any newcomer to speak at least 100 times for free before deciding on whether or not to do it professionally. There's another phrase for it too: "Paying your dues".

I recorded my speech at every opportunity. Especially in the beginning, you need to record your speech as often as you can, at the very least with a digital audio recorder or even better, with a professional camera and crew. Recording your speech gives you a chance to listen to it again yourself. You'll always find small, subtle things to change and improve. Secondarily, it'll give you something to sell. If your message is good, people will want to take it home with them. It creates another source of revenue. Thirdly, if you are going to be a professional, you'll have to have a good demo videotape for potential buyers to preview.

I treated it like a business. Anything that is easy to get into, like network marketing companies, is easy to fail at. Getting into professional speaking appears easy to many. They create a business card and a brochure and wait for the phone to ring. It never happens that way. A business requires a detailed plan for marketing, sales, finances, research and development product creation. A successful business requires sufficient capital to survive the lean years in the beginning. A business requires a professional image that is conveyed through phone systems, voice mail email, web presence, e-commerce, letterhead, business checks, marketing literature, and contracts. An unprofessional image from the start can make the future unlikely.

I invested in quality marketing materials. When I started, I decided that I wanted to eventually be charging at least $5,000 per speech I (even though I started at $500). I called friends within NSA who were currently charging that amount and asked them if they would be willing to send me their marketing materials. They all did. I took their marketing materials to a graphic designer and told him I wanted something that looked the same or better. My first marketing press kit, letterhead and envelopes cost me $5,000. I haven't changed the design in nine years, despite the fact that I now charge more than $13,000 per speech. Invest in quality marketing materials from the beginning and your business will grow faster and you'll save money in the long run by not having to make frequent changes.

Be bureau-friendly. Unless you're one of those rare speakers who never intend to work with bureaus or agents, you have to make your business and marketing materials bureaus-friendly from the start. Successfully working with bureaus can speed your success as a speaker. My business grew exponentially when I started working actively with bureaus.

Customize your speech. Joel Weldon, a very successful speaker and mentor, taught me the importance of customizing my speech for each audience. He showed me how to make my stories relevant to the audience by helping them to overcome a fear, fulfill a need or celebrate a victory. The more work I did to customize my speech to a particular audience, the more repeat business I have gotten over the years. Pacific Bell, a telecommunications giant in California, alone has hired me more than 120 times in the past 3 years. I attribute all of that business to customizing. If you want to learn what Joel taught me, order his "Elephants Still Don't Bite" videocassette from NSA.

Be original. Patricia Fripp, CSP, CPAE once told me to always ask myself, "Has it been said? Can it be said?"

If the stories you're telling have been told by others, or can be told by someone else, get rid of it. I did that years ago and my speech has become completely original. It's the law of supply and demand that has grown my business. I am a limited supply only if I use original stories and therefore my demand grows.

Word of mouth. I figured out a long time ago that the best advertising to do was word of mouth. In the beginning, a lot of companies wanted me to negotiate my fee. They wanted me to speak for less. I was hungrier then. However, I didn't want to give anything away for free anymore, so I settled on a plan. In exchange for lowering my "cash" fee, I wanted them to write five letters of recommendation to their peers or industry leaders recommending me as a speaker at their next event. They were more than happy to do it. Pretty soon, other companies started to call me because I had been recommended.

It takes time. One of the most important things I can end this with is to say that this business, like many good things in life, just takes time. I have found very few things that can leapfrog the place of time in the growing process. Unless you do something that makes you famous or infamous and you appear on the Today show tomorrow, this business takes time and effort to grow. If I had had the perspective from the start, I would have been more patient and enjoyed the ride a little more.

This is a great business. It is satisfying emotionally, intellectually and financially. However, it is not for everyone. If it is right for you, you'll know it. Apply some of the lessons I learned and the journey will be a lot more fun.

Art Berg CSP, CPAE

On December 26, 1983, at the age of 21, Art Berg broke his neck in a car accident. This left him a quadriplegic. In spite of this, Art earned three national sales awards as a computer salesman for a national firm and became president of Invictus Communications, Inc. He was named Young Entrepreneur of the year by the Small Business Administration. Art Berg was a world-class wheelchair athlete across variety of sports. In 1993 he set a world record by becoming the first quadriplegic to race in an ultra marathon of 325 miles.

Art passed away in 2002.

❝ ❞ Quotes On Speaking

If you don't know what you want to achieve in your presentation your audience never will.

Harvey Diamond

The best way to conquer stage fright is to know what you're talking about.

Michael H. Mescon

I have a genuine love affair with my audience. When I'm on stage they're not privileged to see me. It's a privilege for me to see them.

Ozzy Osbourne

AWARD WINNING SPEAKER

Jeff Blackman, J.D., CSP, CPAE

1. Focus on delivering value and results. Focus on the outcomes and benefits of your message, not merely what your message is about.

2. Scour your local paper for meetings that are likely to hire speakers, even if it's for no fee or minimal fee. In the beginning you want an "audience" to hone your craft. Even if it's for a small fee, request that the "fee" instead be used as a donation to your/their favorite charity. This removes any economic motivation for you or economic deterrent for your decision maker. However, request other things of value, i.e., a membership list, the opportunity to write on-going articles for their newsletter, etc.

3. Develop some type of "leave behind" so that audience members can easily contact you. It can be as simple as "key points from your program" on your letterhead.

4. Ask for referrals, all the time.

5. Develop "business-growth tools" (a.k.a. products) that will complement your message. And, do it early in your career.

6. Show up early. Stay late. Network with people. This will be a driving force for your future success.

7. Be more interested in other folks and their problems, challenges, hopes and dreams. They are not real interested in what "you speak on"...unless it will have some positive impact on their personal or professional life.

8. Remember, the only thing other human beings want...is a more favorable future. If you help them attain it...you'll succeed beyond your wildest dreams!

Jeff Blackman, J.D., CSP, CPAE
Business-Growth Specialist
Speaker • Author • Coach • Broadcaster • Lawyer
jeff@jeffblackman.com
www.jeffblackman.com
847.998.0688
Blackman & Associates, Inc.
2130 Warwick Lane
Glenview, IL 60025

Jeff is the author of:

RESULT$ • (book • Successories)

Peak Your Profits • (book • Victory Books)

How to Set and Really Achieve Your Goals • (video • JWA Video)

Profitable Customer Service • (video • JWA Video)

Opportunity $elling® / Six Profit-Producing Steps to Multiply Your Earnings • (audio • POPP Publishing)

Opportunity $elling® • (sales/quotation book • Prosperity Press)

He also hosts the TV talk-show: INSIGHT

" " Quotes On Speaking

90% of how well the talk will go is determined before the speaker steps on the platform.

Somers White

The perception of the audience is the interesting part. If the audience doesn't hear what is going on, is it going on or not?

Robert Fripp

I love the rehearsal process in the theatre, and the visceral sense of contact and communication with a live audience.

Judd Nelson

How To Turn A Service Club Talk Into A Marketing Opportunity

AWARD WINNING SPEAKER

Patricia Fripp, CSP, CPAE

Speaking before a group about your business is definitely the lowest cost and best way to market your product or service and expand your customer base. From firsthand experience I learned this important marketing lesson. I started talking about my hair styling business at local service organizations, such as Rotary, Kiwanis, Optimists. At the time I didn't have much public speaking experience beyond Dale Carnegie courses and Toastmasters. Little did I know it would lead to a rewarding career as an executive speech coach and keynote speaker. Here are some key points I learned that helped me build my business.

Expressing yourself with flair will increase the speed with which you succeed.

Peter Butler is an excellent example of how to increase your reputation and visibility by speaking. Peter was in the insurance and financial services industry. When he passed his fiftieth birthday, he decided to start running in Iron Man triathlons and other athletic events around the country.

He gave lively talks at service clubs about his experiences. Peter starts by saying, "Running a marathon is like planning for your future." Then he told colorful stories about the different events he had participated in. Finally he said, "For my last few minutes, here are four ideas you should know about planning for your long-term future."

Notice that his speech is not a sales presentation-yet it actually is. The audience starts out knowing all about his business credentials because the club official who introduces him has read them from an introduction that Peter provided. (This is standard procedure for all speakers.) Then Peter's introductory remark related his business (preparing for the future financially) to his topic (preparing for a marathon). His final minutes were his philosophy. He was tremendously effective, and people stood in line afterwards to get his business card.

Visibility is necessary for success in almost any business.

My executive speech coaching client Michael Sipe brought home to me the tremendous difference between building a business vs. having a job working for yourself. Mike is a mergers and acquisitions specialist, arranging and negotiating the sale of (you guessed it) businesses. One of his clients was Bob. His example was so vivid his audience could totally relate to both Bob and Mike. They understood that having all your contacts and strategies in your head would never make your business saleable.

Check out the Room:

Being prepared is a key to presenting a good talk. It's a comfort knowing that the lights, the microphone, and the projector are working and, more importantly, that you know how to work with them.

Go to the room where you will be speaking earlier than everybody else. Imagine yourself a success. Get comfortable on the stage. Test the microphone. Are your notes in order? You may not be a professional speaker, but struggling with audio/visual equipment just distracts and annoys your audience. You want them on your side.

Presenting your Talk:

Do not read your speech. Take your key points in 20-24 point type you keep on the lectern or table on the podium. I urge you not to stand behind the lectern throughout your entire talk. It puts a barrier between you and the audience and they feel it. However, if you feel more secure standing behind the lectern, do not lean on it.

The Introduction:

Write your own introduction. Use your resume as a guide, but customize it to fit the topic on which you're speaking. Do not include your job as a lifeguard in your intro unless it directly relates to your subject.

Handouts:

Develop a page detailing your key points. Or if you've had an article published, make copies for the audience members. Make sure that the handout includes your name, email and telephone number.

Business Cards:

If your goal is to develop business contacts, always collect business cards from the audience members. You can offer to send additional information, articles or tip sheets to them. Or you can offer a door prize (this can be a product you sell or certificate for service–a free evaluation of financial status, etc.); ask that everyone drop their business cards in a box from which you or the program chair will draw the winner (or winners) at the end of your talk. The business cards give you prospects with whom you can follow up later.

Just Do It!

Speaking before a group of strangers can be intimidating, but keep focused on the positive impact the presentation will have on your business reputation and your bottom line. Don't expect to be a magnificent speaker the first time out. Your goal is to present the most valuable information possible to the members of the audience. Think of it as the beginning of many long-term relationships.

Go on–step up on the podium and profit from the experience.

Reprinted with permission from:

www.fripp.com/category/fripp-articles

Patricia Fripp, CSP, CPAE is an award-winning speaker, author, sales presentation skills trainer and in-demand speech coach. Her speech-coaching clients include corporate leaders, celebrity speakers, well-known sports and media personalities, ministers, and sales teams. Meetings and Conventions magazine named her "One of the 10 most electrifying speakers in North America." She delivers high-energy, high-content, and dramatically memorable presentations.

Kiplinger's Personal Finance named her speaking school the sixth best way to invest in your career.

The over 4,000-member National Speakers Association elected her the first female President in 1984. She has been awarded NSA's Hall of Fame and the Cavett Award, the highest honor and considered the Oscar of the speaking world.

Patricia founded and was President of the largest National Speakers Association chapter, NSA Northern California. Patricia is also a member of NSA Las Vegas and has donated her time to speak at more NSA chapters than any other leader in the history of NSA.

Patricia Fripp is the author of two books, Get What You Want! and Make It, So You Don't Have to Fake It!, and coauthor of Speaking Secrets of the Masters and Insights into Excellence. She is featured in the Bullet Proof Manager video series, which is sold in over fifty countries.

Patricia is a member of the prestigious Speakers Roundtable. The members of Speakers Roundtable are a "Who's Who" of experts and Hall of Fame professional speakers.

Patricia Fripp, CSP, CPAE, Cavett Award winner
A Speaker for All Reasons™
527 Hugo Street
San Francisco, CA
94122 USA
Telephone: (415) 753-6556
Fax: (415) 753-0914
pfripp@ix.netcom.com
www.fripp.com

" "
Quotes On Speaking

If you can't explain it simply, you don't understand it well enough.

Albert Einstein

Speech is the mirror of the soul;
as a man speaks, so he is.

Publilius Syrus

The last thing I'd learn, well into my career,
was how to get on, how to say hello,
how to get in with the audience.

Phyllis Diller

AWARD WINNING SPEAKER

Roger E. Herman, CSP, CMC

Opportunities abound for associations and corporations, locally, at the state-level, nationally, and internationally. Work your way up by paying your dues at each level. Give lots of free speeches to refine your skills, build your confidence, and gain valuable exposure. Don't put your business cards or brochures at everyone's seat; that's blatant marketing and will turn people off. Instead, give them note-taking pages or sheets with additional information about your topic, and put your name, address, phone number, e-mail address, and website at the bottom of the page. Be subtle.

Connect with your audience by putting yourself in their shoes. Understand what they would like to learn, what they would like to take away after spending time with you. It's helpful to actually sit in their chairs before the program. See how you will look from the audience's perspective, and experience what your audience will feel. What would you want if you were in their place?

Attend chapter and national meetings of the National Speakers Association to see the masters at work. Carefully observe their techniques to see how they use language, inflection, presence, gestures, pauses, and all the other skills of the professional speaker. Practice those skills yourself, weaving into your presentation the technical aspects that feel right for you.

Don't invest a tremendous amount of money in fancy promotional pieces. Flash doesn't sell; content and reputation sell. Record your presentations so you will have tapes--audio and video--to send prospective clients. As you get started, audiotapes will probably be sufficient. As you move up in the field, seeking more desirable--and lucrative--engagements, you'll need a professionally done video. Don't use a non-professional video; you'll be compared against speakers with professional videos, and you'll probably lose. Go after those engagements you believe you can win. Gradually go after the others that are more of a stretch.

A website is essential in today's marketplace. Work with a professional, rather than trying to create something yourself. This is your image. Visit the websites of other speakers, particularly your competitors and potential competitors as you consider design and positioning. Be sure your e-mail address has your domain name, rather than AOL, Yahoo, or some other internet service provider. Demonstrate your positioning by being good enough to have your own domain.

Write articles. Always add a bio at the end of your articles, telling readers how they can reach you. The articles should be demonstrations of your expertise in your chosen subject area. Write a book, again on-target with your expertise. The alignment between your writing and speaking will serve you well. Remember, the most successful speakers are experts who speak, not just speakers.

Roger E. Herman, CSP, CMC
The Herman Group
www.hermangroup.com
7112 Viridian Lane Austin, TX 78739
Voice: 336-210-3547

Roger Herman was a futurist, businessman and professional speaker. He was an expert on workforce and workplace trends. He helps corporate leaders see and understand those trends and prepare for their impacts. He wrote 11 books. He was the Contributing Editor, Workforce & Workplace Trends, for The Futurist Magazine.

Designations:

- Certified Speaking Professional (CSP), by the National Speakers Association

- Certified Management Consultant, by the Institute of Management Consultants

- 31st Fellow of the Institute of Management Consultants

Memberships:

- Founding Member, Association of Professional Futurists

- World Future Society (Professional Member)

- Society for Human Resource Management

- National Speakers Association (Professional Member)

- Institute of Management Consultants

- Mensa

Roger passed away in 2006.

" " Quotes On Speaking

Look your audience straight in the eyes, and begin to talk as if every one of them owed you money.

Dale Carnegie

Effective communication is 20% what you know and 80% how you feel about what you know.

Jim Rohn

Like I always tell people, I don't pander to any audience, but you have to play to your audience.

Gary Owens

Dr. Willie Jolley, CSP, CPAE

1. Take a Toastmasters Course, even if you are already speaking the short six week course can help you to better craft your speech.

2. Attend a meeting of the National Speakers Association (either a local meeting or a national meeting). It will tremendously help cut your learning curve.

3. Tape every speech. You will learn as you listen, plus one of those speeches will be the "magic speech" and will become your first audio product.

4. Talk for and to lots of people. Talk for as many people as you can, and always give away something (your card, a handout, a bookmarker) because those people will in time become your marketing team. Also talk to as many people as you can and let them know what you are doing and what your message is all about. You will be surprised what business opportunities come from just talking to lots of people.

5. Always remember to have fun and stay focused on inspiring the audience, and not just impressing them. Not only will it help you to be audience entered but it will take away a lot of your nervousness.

Dr. Willie Jolley, CSP, CPAE
President/CEO of Willie Jolley Worldwide

Chosen "One of the Outstanding Five Speakers In The World!" By The 170,000 Members Of Toastmasters International (1999)

Author of the National Bestseller, "It Only Takes A Minute To Change Your Life!" and the book "A Setback is A Setup for A Comeback!"

Host of the Motivational Minute Audio-line, (Free Minute of Motivation): 1-888-266-8488

Phone: 202-723-8863 / 800-487-8899 / Fax: 202-722-1180
P.O. Box 55459, Washington DC 20040
Willie Jolley-Not just a Speech, but an Experience!
Website: www.williejolley.com

Dr. Willie Jolley is a world-class, award-winning speaker and singer, best-selling author and media personality. Willie holds a Doctorate of Ministry Degree in Faith Driven Achievement from the California Graduate School of Theology, a Master's Degree in Theology from Wesley Theological seminary and a B.A. in Psychology and Sociology from The American University.

Quotes On Speaking

It is with words as with sunbeams. The more they are condensed, the deeper they burn.

Robert Southey

What is powerful is when what you say is just the tip of the iceberg of what you know.

Jim Rohn

I've always had to conquer fear when I'm on stage. Basically, I was and still am a very shy person. It's absolutely in conflict with what I do. But once I deliver the first joke I'm okay.

Steven Wright

Professional Speakers: Building Your Business Without Working More

AWARD WINNING SPEAKER

Peter Legge, O.B.C., LL.D. (HON.), D.Tech., CSP, CPAE, Hall Of Fame Author & Professional Speaker

Building your business without working more is a bit of an oxymoron. After all, the very process of building a business requires long hours and hard work. However, the process should not be to the detriment to your family, health or personal life. Working more means spending the hours wisely - concentrating your efforts on the things that are really important, including devoting some of your time to making a difference in the world.

So, where do we begin? Well, I believe it all begins with recognizing your talents and using them - a lesson I uncovered near the end of a book that my children gave me for Father's Day - Hillary Rodham Clinton's Living History. Clinton wrote that she was wondering if she should run for Senator for the State of New York. As she agonized over the difficult decision she received a letter from her friend, Father Tribou, who wrote:

"Dear Hillary: I want to tell you what I have been telling students for 50 years. It is my opinion on Judgment Day that the first question God asks is not about the Ten Commandments (although he gets to that later) but he asks each of us this; 'What did you do with the time and the talents I gave you?' Bottom line, Hillary - run!" Signed Father Tribou.

Hillary Clinton did run for office and won. Father Tribou reminds us of our responsibility to identify and develop our talents. That same wisdom is reflected in the words of Denis Waitley, who said, "We are all born with the seeds of greatness." All of us possess potential, however, it is up to us to plant and nurture those seeds of possibility.

We as professional speakers are indeed fortunate to be working in a world where there is a growing demand for those whose talents lie in motivating and inspiring others. Bill Emmett, editor of The Economist and author of the best-selling book 2021, asserts that the world is in better shape today than it has ever been and that it is improving by the minute. Why? Because most people want to be more successful at their careers and are committed to improving their social situation.

It is part of our role as professional speakers to be the champions of the possibilities life has to offer. In fact, encouraging, inspiring and guiding people along the path to building a better life are central themes of most presentations from the platform. While few would argue that a career as a professional speaker is interesting and rewarding, there is a cost, because as we improve and enjoy greater success in our chosen profession, we are naturally asked to do more speaking. Perhaps Walt Disney summed up the ramping-up effect of success best when he said, "Do what you do so well so that when other people see what it is you do they will want to see you do it again and they will bring others with them to show them what it is that you do."

So how do you build your business without necessarily working more?

It is important to begin by acknowledging the fact that successful people do work long hours - it is unavoidable. That said, however, it is what you do with that time that is important. To that end, I believe the key to achieving more without necessarily working more is establishing balance in your life - and also in your own character. You don't want to be so single-minded in purpose that you forsake everything else in your life. You don't want to be so rich and have such a negative attitude that nobody wants to live with you. Nor do you want to be so poor that you spend all your time worrying about the mortgage and putting food on the table. No matter what kind of hours you work, strive for balance in your life. Make time for work, play, friends, family and time for you.

It simply isn't possible do everything, so it is critical that you prioritize what is important. Further, I think, it is vital that you recognize your most significant gifts and that you focus on developing them. Remember, there are only 24 hours in the day. Commit your available time to developing your best abilities and guard against wasting precious hours on areas that are no longer viable. You will be more productive when you train your energies on using your very best talents.

Silent income from books, booklets, tapes and articles can reduce your workload, however, the better you become as a professional speaker, the more in demand you will become, which brings me back to the critical importance of balance. If you can learn that all your work is not really work but an adventure in living, you can build your business and your life side by side.

I don't believe we can be successful unless other people want us to be, and I also don't believe we can maximize our potential by working from nine to five. Most successful business leaders work 60 to 85 hours a week. So better enjoy what you do. Remember Father Tribou -"What did you do with the time and talents I gave you?" How do you answer this question?

Peter Legge is a member of Speakers Roundtable with Patricia Fripp and one of Canada's greatest philanthropists and most in-demand speakers: www.speakersroundtable.com

Peter Legge, O.B.C., LL.D. (HON.), D.Tech., CSP, CPAE, HoF is Chairman and CEO of Canada Wide Media Limited, the largest independently owned magazine publishing company in Western Canada controlling a network of over 25 magazines across the country in addition to providing a diverse range of media services and products with over $15 million in sales annually.

Peter has received the Golden Gavel Award from Toastmasters International and was voted "Top Speaker in North America." Peter has been presented with two Honorary Doctor of Laws Degrees - one from Simon Fraser University in 2003, and the other from Royal Roads University in 2009. In 2010, Peter received an Honorary Doctorate of Technology from BCIT.

In 2003, the Canadian Professional Sales Association inducted Peter into the Sales Hall of Fame. Peter has also been inducted into the Speakers Hall of Fame by both the National Speakers Association in the United States and the Canadian Association of Professional Speakers, and was appointed as one of the Ambassadors for the 2010 Winter Olympic Games.

❝ ❞ Quotes On Speaking

You can be accessible
without catering to an audience.

Halsey

I'm not performing anymore. I reveal myself to the
audience. I reveal myself.
That's the show now.

Eddie Murphy

Your purpose is to make your audience see what you
saw, hear what you heard, feel what you felt. Relevant
detail, couched in concrete, colorful language, is the
best way to recreate the incident as it happened and to
picture it for the audience.

Dale Carnegie

AWARD WINNING SPEAKER

Grady Jim Robinson, CSP, CPAE

In the early days of my speaking career I made a tape, one tape, of a speech I had made and walked it into the office of Top Billing in Nashville Tennessee. They liked it and said send me your stuff. I didn't have any stuff. Here's a tip: don't attempt to do things in your career that you are not ready to do. Allow it to flow at a natural pace.

In the early days of my career I had made about a dozen free speeches without much success. After attending an NSA workshop I realized that every speaker I'd heard used a lot of humor. For my next speech at the Kirkwood Rotary Club I prepared a lot of fun material, jokes, a story or two about growing up in Arkansas, something out of the headlines of the paper. The speech was a rousing success and I was asked to do five speeches from those 75 audience members. Tip: A successful speaker is wise to use sizzle to entertain listeners. Humor is the best means of sizzle for a speaker.

Develop personal stories. Personal stories are self-revealing that bond speaker and listener. Your stories will grow and soon become signature stories that can be used as metaphors and adapted to every audience. Tip: Explore the power of stories.

Grady Jim Robinson, CSP, CPAE
www.nwaonline.com/staff/grady-jim-robinson
www.brooksinternational.com/GradyJimRobinson_951.htm
Brooks International

763 Santa Fe Drive
Denver, CO 80204
303-825-8700

Grady Jim Robinson is a writer, humorist, and storyteller who has been captivating audiences for decades. His talents as a speaker have earned him a place in the National Speakers Association Hall of Fame. He has been both a minister and standup comic and ultimately became a fulltime professional speaker and freelance writer. He has written radio scripts for legendary speakers Art Linkletter and Zig Ziglar. He also wrote a popular column for the St. Louis Globe-Democrat.

❝ ❞ Quotes On Speaking

To get an Oscar would be an incredible moment in my career, there is no doubt about that. But the 'Lord of the Rings' films are not made for Oscars, they are made for the audience.

Peter Jackson

I work hard for the audience. It's entertainment. I don't need validation.

Denzel Washington

The only people with power today are the audience. And that is increasing with Twitter, Facebook, and everything else. We cater to their likes and dislikes, and you ignore that at your peril.

Simon Cowell

147

AWARD WINNING SPEAKER

Lorna Riley, CSP

Professional speaking is the most thrilling and rewarding career I can recommend because you can reach the most number of people in the shortest time through speeches, training and books. If you are passionate about your message--leave your fear on the side of the road and make the first step.

1. What are you passionate about? Build your career about what you think is an important message or skill. It will sustain you in the tough times when you wonder what and why you've chosen this profession.

2. Create a vision of your future. Where do who you see yourself in five years? Standing on a stage? In a training room? Lecturing around the world? Describe a typical ideal day in writing.

3. Decide on a company name that reflects your focus.

4. Create your topic list.

5. Write your programs. If a speech, start by writing a 30-45 minute talk. If you're unsure how to do this, join Toastmasters or reach one of the many helpful speech writing books out there.

6. Start speaking to groups and videotaping every talk. Can start with your Chamber of Commerce's list of local clubs. Call the program chair for each club and find out what they look for in a speaker. Ask to become part of their program.

7. Get testimonial letters from every talk.

8. Create your press kit.

9. Call local companies out of the phone book. Offer free programs and more if they like.

What is your USP? Unique Selling Proposition? Why would someone do business with you instead of your competition? What topics are people paying to learn more about? How can you leverage what you're passionate about into those topics people will pay to hear? I'm passionate about the heroic journey. No one asks for this topic directly, but I've given it "corporate friendly " language and talk about getting results as a leader, top sales performer, change manager etc. by using the process of becoming a hero. I don't tell audiences about the heroic process until the end of the program, after I've got buy-in. Then they're delighted to have their awareness expanded.

Practice does not make perfect. Perfect practice makes perfect. Videotape your presentations, get feedback from others and practice perfectly until the material is part of your blood stream. If you can, hire a coach to pick your speech apart. You must completely own the material before you can be in flow with it and your audience.

I have a fee structure for keynotes, and a different one for training since they go through different departments and I do both. I've found that if you ask for what you think you and your material is worth, and you really believe it's worth your fee, you will get it. Believing in the importance of your offering is the first step in getting comfortable with being paid thousands of dollars for a few minutes of your time.

Before quoting your fees, ask what their fee range is. You may find the quote way above or below your price point and can save a lot of time in your negotiations. If the quote is below your fee, see if you can do several programs to increase the fee. If above, offer product or additional services to compensate for the difference.

Get someone to make the calls for you so you can spend your time growing roots and developing yourself and your products. Otherwise, your business will never grow to the level where you are being sought after for your knowledge or uniqueness.

Just write. Spend at least an hour a day writing something--articles, book chapters. It forces you to amass a body of work that will someday be a reflection of your life's work. Without it, you are left with thin air and some plaques on the wall. Spoken, unrecorded words are fleeting. Capture your work in something tangible. You'll want some evidence of your efforts.

Lorna Riley, CSP
American Training Association
888-530-7983
2455 Flametree Lane, Vista, CA 92084
lorna@lornariley.com
www.lornariley.com

Creator of the acclaimed "Quest for Your Best" and "Off-the-Chart Results"

Author: Quest for Your Best, Achieving Results: Four Stages to Excellence In A Changing World, 76 Ways to Build a Straight Referral Business.

Lorna Riley is the founder and CEO Chart Learning Solutions, a leader in developing high- performance. As a 28-year veteran international professional speaker, trainer, author, and consultant, she conducts high-impact programs that inspire a passion for continuous growth and excellence. She has an award-winning background in sales, banking, printing, advertising, marketing, education, and music.

Winner--Brandon Hall Award: Best Results from a Learning Program

Winner--Brandon Hall Award: Best Use of Blended Learning

Winner--American Business Award: Best Training Website

American Society of Training and Development PEAK Award

Winner—Consummate Speaker Award

Winner—National Speaker Association Gold Microphone Award

" " Quotes On Speaking

A speech is a solemn responsibility. The man who makes a bad thirty-minute speech to two hundred people waste only a half hour of his own time. But he wastes one hundred hours of the audience's time - more than four days-which should be a hanging offense.

Jenkin Lloyd Jones

A man never becomes an orator
if he has anything to say.

Finley Peter Dunne

What orators lack in depth
they make up for in length.

Baron de Montesquieu

Working with
Meeting Planners
And Attendees

Quotes On Speaking

Condense some daily experience into a glowing symbol
and an audience is electrified.

Ralph Waldo Emerson

Every speaker has a mouth; An arrangement rather
neat. Sometimes it's filled with wisdom. Sometimes it's
filled with feet.

Robert Orben

Every time you have to speak,
you are auditioning for leadership.

James Humes

The 47 Most Common Complaints Meeting Planners Have About Professional Speakers

Bill Cole, MS, MA

Having the perfect speaker can make the difference between your meeting being a dream or being a nightmare.

If you hire professional speakers, you know things can sometimes go wrong, even with the best, most professional speakers. That's why you want to eliminate basic meeting mistakes that just don't need to occur. Hire the wrong speaker, and your headaches will only multiply.

There is a saying, "No speaker is perfect, but when things go wrong at a meeting, an experienced speaker's abilities come to the fore and save the day".

There is another saying, "Smart speakers don't make basic, dumb speaking mistakes". But inexperienced speakers can make dumb mistakes. Those mistakes can be costly. Fortunately, if you hire the right speaker they don't have to be made.

I've witnessed many of these goofs. I was a meeting planner when I was on the Board of Directors for the National Speakers Association in Northern California. I helped hire speakers, promote them, organize their room and AV set-up, introduce them and rate them. I still help clients run their meetings where I speak.

This is what meeting planners and audiences complain about when it comes to speakers who do not know what they are doing. The speaker can make these critical gaffs that can ruin the entire audience experience.

Here are the 47 most common errors speakers can make before, during and after a presentation.

1. Little or no research on the audience's needs and wants.

2. Little or no understanding of the meetings industry.

3. Little or no understanding of the audience's industry.

4. Doesn't understand the meeting objectives.

5. Doesn't understand their role in the meeting.

6. Shows up late or at the last minute.

7. No room or AV preparation.

8. Gets in the way of the meeting planner.

9. Fails to meet and greet the audience in advance.

10. Fails to create rapport with the audience.

11. Unavailable by phone, fax or email.

12. Demanding and big ego.

13. Inflexible when problems come up.

14. Unprofessional behavior and image off-stage.

15. No interest in meeting the people in your organization off-stage.

16. Unethical behavior.

17. No coordination of message with prior speakers.

18. Insults the audience through sex-ism, gender-ism, class-ism, age-ism, race-ism, size-ism, etc.

19. Insults the audience, sponsors or meeting planner.

20. Gives a book report, not engaging material.

21. Fluff-based content, with no real research or meaningful data.

22. All style and no substance.

23. Gives an off-the-shelf talk when a custom speech was promised.

24. The audience does nothing but sit.

25. Few or no audience interaction techniques.

26. Falls victim to stage fright.

27. Has no Q and A period or handles it poorly.

28. Poor handouts or none at all.

29. Makes no emotional or intellectual connection with the audience.

30. Doesn't support the meeting themes and messages.

31. Uses weak humor, or has none at all.

32. Inappropriate, insulting use of humor.

33. Speaks far over or under the knowledge level of the audience.

34. Tired, old content.

35. Tells few stories or none at all-they are nothing but data and facts.

36. Uses other people's stories or old ones.

37. Uses content that is not applicable to the audience's challenges.

38. Does not help the audience transfer the speech material to their particular pragmatic needs.

39. Lack of respect for audience members.

40. Not ADA or OSHA aware or compliant.

41. Under-uses or over-uses technology.

42. Sells product when inappropriate.

43. Does not take leadership, especially in an emergency.

44. Leaves immediately after the presentation.

45. Does not clear the stage quickly for the next speaker.

46. Does not speak with the meeting planner, post-talk, for feedback purposes.

47. Takes the check and runs.

Speakers who make mistakes like these can ruin a meeting. They may be all about themselves, and have demanding egos. They may simply be inexperienced. They may have low awareness of how to make a meeting special. Worse, perhaps they don't even care.

Whatever the reason, it's important to hire experienced speakers who provide a "pledge of services" so you know what you are getting.

Hire the right speaker and your meeting nightmares will be replaced with sweet dreams.

❝ ❞ Quotes On Speaking

Great is our admiration of the orator who speaks with
fluency and discretion.

Marcus T. Cicero

Most speakers speak ten minutes too long.

James Humes

Passions are the only orators
to always convince us.

Francois De La Rochefoucauld

The 46 Most Common "Meeting Monsters" Presenters Encounter

Bill Cole, MS, MA

What is your worst nightmare as a speaker, trainer, facilitator or teacher? You're presenting, and you notice that things are not going so well. You realize you are being interrupted, disrupted, distracted, insulted, slowed down, hurried, side-tracked and stymied. Who is doing this? Your audience!

Yes, even though the lights are on during your presentation, you will bump into many scary monsters. Characters. Odd behaving creatures.

Who are these meeting monsters?

These are the folks who annoy, stall, stop and ruin a meeting, speech or team event. They upset your flow as a speaker. They throw a monkey wrench into the meeting works.

Are they odd, weird human beings? Or is this just called the wonderful and mysterious human condition? Guess what? It's normal.

People in your audience bring all their human foibles to every presentation. These personal peccadilloes will arise, to some degree, in every meeting you attend.

People are wonderful, yet they can be challenging in a meeting setting. Group dynamics and historical and current personal psychology are at work, and just because you wish your audience to behave a certain way, there is no guarantee of that happening. Not unless you know what to do when problems arise. And they will arise.

What to do?

First, become aware of these wonderful characters and their ways. Then devise ways to counter their moves.

Your job as the leader (presenter, teacher, speaker) is to recognize these types, have a strategic plan ready, and handle them with tact, diplomacy and aplomb. Then, your meeting will move along smoothly, and you will have mitigated the quirky speed bumps called meeting monsters.

Here are the 46 most typical meeting monsters you will encounter in your presentations. Know them by name.

1. **High Tech Hugh.** He brings a beeper, laptop and an entire collection of electronic gadgetry. He's sad he can't bring more.

2. **Cell Phone Phil.** He's never out of touch with friends.

3. **Cary The Captive.** He is held in class against his will.

4. **Prove-It Pete.** He's a major skeptic who needs proof on everything.

5. **Chit-Chat Charlie.** He never stops talking. It's a disease.

6. **Teacher's Pet Paula.** She is forever trying to make an impression on the teacher.

7. **Silent Sandra.** She won't respond or react to a word you are saying. She's a mystery woman. Check her pulse.

8. **Tommy Turn-Off.** He closes up and turns off. You can't get him to participate in group activities on a bet.

9. **Unsafe Susan.** She's a walking train wreck in group activities. An accident waiting to happen. Make sure you have 911 on speed-dial.

10. **Bored Bob.** All you see of Bob is his open mouth, yawning.

11. **Needy Nancy.** She never seems to have what she needs, and is always asking you to provide for her.

12. **Questioning Quentin.** He asks non-stop questions. And expects answers.

13. **Jerry The Judge.** He passes judgment on everything you do and say, and announces his "findings" to the "court" at will.

14. **High Helen.** By drink or by drug, Helen alters her consciousness.

15. **Take-Over Tim.** Tim tells you how to run the class, give the speech, arrange the room, etc.

16. **Dave The Dominator.** He takes over every discussion and wants to be the boss.

17. **Dumb Question Don.** Don stays awake at night to come up with the most basic, obvious questions he can invent. Then he asks them.

18. **Dan the Doodler.** He thinks he's in art class.

19. **Note Passing Ned.** He thinks he's in junior high.

20. **Hostile Hal.** Hal has a chip on his shoulder, and he dares you to knock it off.

21. **Victor The Volunteer.** He raises his hand for everything. He wants to be involved, always. No one else gets a chance.

22. **Paranoid Patrick.** He feels attacked by everyone and everything. He also attacks back.

23. **Kerry The Caterer.** She brings a seven-course meal to every meeting. Sounds and sights included.

24. **Orville The Offender.** He insults entire classes of people-by race, age, size, gender, religion, etc. He's an all-inclusive, equal opportunity insult artist.

25. **Pop-Up Pat.** She just can't sit still. Every other minute she's out of her chair, going here, going there. Decaf, Pat.

26. **Jeff The Jeweler.** Jeff goes jingle-jangle with his watch, bracelet, necklace, briefcase, pen, pencil and anything else he can grab.

27. **Barry the Bully.** Barry never met a person he couldn't intimidate.

28. **Humorous Helen.** Helen has a joke for every occasion...and will be glad to tell it.

29. **Late Larry.** He never arrives on time. And he's proud of it.

30. **Mark Micro Man.** Mark is a detail freak extraordinaire. He will fuss-budget you to death.

31. **Snoozing Sam.** See Sam sleep. See Sam snore.

32. **Harry the Hurry-Upper.** He's in a rush to get things moving. Or to end the meeting. He'll hurry you, too.

33. **One-Better Ben.** He always can one-up anyone. He has a better idea, a better way, a better comment. He'll share them too.

34. **Yes-But Betty.** She always says "Yes, but..." and then finds 25 reasons to dash your ideas and suggestions. For Betty, there are no good solutions.

35. **Protocol Paul.** Thinks he co-wrote the book on meeting etiquette, called Robert's Rules. Wanted it named Paul's Rules.

36. **No-Manners Mary.** If Mary can offend, she will. Intentionally or not.

37. **Irene The Indecisive.** Irene is still making her mind up from an event that happened ten years ago.

38. **Side-Talking Tom.** Tom can face straight ahead, yet carry on a side conversation at 90 degrees. He does so often.

39. **Iris The Impresser.** She wants to wow everyone, every time she speaks.

40. **William The Whiny.** He annoys people with his non-stop complaints and troubles.

41. **Carol The Corrector.** Don't worry, if you make even the slightest mistake, Carol will be glad to tell everyone what you did or said wrong. She'll even help you fix it.

42. **Smart-Guy Gary.** He is the original know it all, and he'll tell you so.

43. **Oppositional Ollie.** He plays Devil's Advocate to everything you say. Even if you say nothing. Try it and see.

44. **Side-Issue Steve.** Steve steers the discussion to the left or right, up or down, and sometimes inside or out, anytime he can. He's a regular roller-coaster.

45. **Heckling Hector.** He has a snappy come-back one-liner insult for everything you say. Should have his own HBO special. Is often mistaken for Don Rickles.

46. **Hypothetical Harold.** He goes off into La-La Land to invent improbable, impossible scenarios to ask you about. And he expects a straight answer.

How many of these meeting monsters do you recognize? See yourself anywhere in this list? You will never have a room full of "perfect" students or audience members. After all, people are human. They will do what they will, and what they can. Your job as the leader is to recognize these denizens of the deep and respond to them with grace, polish and control so your presentation runs smoothly and you achieve the results you envisioned.

Want to know how to handle each of these characters? Work with a speech coach to create effective measures to counter each move the meeting monsters make. You can do so without appearing to "control" people or the situation. Instead, you'll come off as experienced and savvy, and as a sharp leader who has it all together. Your audience will thank you for it.

Quotes On Speaking

I've experienced plenty of times when something I think is funny doesn't do very well. And there are times when something I don't think is funny makes the audience laugh so hard.

Carrot Top

There's something about being in front of a live audience that's fun. It's a really interesting, very electric, very alive, and intense experience, and you can't get it anywhere else. And I've been doing it since I was 23, so it's part of my being. It's part of my fabric as a person.

Steven Wright

You have to respect your audience.
Without them, you're essentially
standing alone, singing to yourself.

K. D. Lang

Resources For Professional Development

" " Quotes On Speaking

I was always more interested in the ultimate live
performance rather than the recording
for its own sake. And, for the audience too,
that thrill of just being there.

Ian Anderson

I do miss the rhythms of comedy. And I've never been
able to perform very well without an audience. The
sitcoms I've done had them.
It was like doing a little play.

Dick Van Dyke

I'm really only happy when I'm on stage. I just feed off
the energy of the audience. That's what I'm all about -
people and laughter.

Larry David

The National Speakers Association

We strongly suggest you look into the National Speakers Association, for many reasons. NSA is the premier professional society for public speakers or aspiring public speakers. This is an organization that can shorten your learning curve immensely in this business.

NSA operates on the foundation of three core values: sharing, serving and mentoring.

1. Expertise: Professional speakers truly know their subject matter.

2. Eloquence: Professional speakers are masters at delivering what they know to inspire audiences.

3. Enterprise: Professional speakers know how to make a living through their speaking platform.

4. Ethics: Professional speakers believe that the actions of one NSA member reflects on all NSA members, and they are therefore expected to uphold a clear set of ethical guidelines.

Membership In NSA

NSA has six primary designations for membership. This makes it possible for people of varying experience levels to join and immediately qualify for educational resources, events and networking.

1. Academy Membership: This entry-level membership is for aspiring professional speakers who are just getting started in the professional speaking

173

business. Academy members receive discounted pricing to the annual one-day Cavett Institute, subscriptions to Speaker magazine and the Voices of Experience® audio magazine, monthly eLearning opportunities, discounts on NSA national events, and additional benefits.

2. Qualified Professional Membership: Requirements for this membership level include one of the following criteria: Provide supporting documentation that you have received compensation for 20 or more presentations, or that you have given 20 or more presentations to audiences of 15 or more as part of a salaried position, or that you have earned $25,000 or more giving presentations. Any of these have to have been within the 12 months prior to application.

3. Certified Professional Member: Professional members of NSA are also eligible to earn a certification that require additional rigor. The CSP designation or Certified Professional Speaker is the speaking profession's international measure of professional platform competence. A little over 10-12 percent of the 5,000 plus professional NSA speakers worldwide currently hold this professional designation. These folks are recognized as being one of the best in this field.

4. Council of Peers Award for Excellence (CPAE): The Council of Peers Award for Excellence Speaker Hall of Fame® (CPAE) is an award for speaking excellence and professionalism given to speakers who have mastered seven categories: professionalism, material, image, style, experience, delivery, and communication.

5. Professional Affiliate Membership: This is a membership for businesses that support professional speakers, NSA or speaking bureaus.

6. Student Membership: This is for students who aspire to be a professional speaker. These are typically high school or college students.

The Benefits Of Joining NSA

1. Here are just some of the benefits you'll get when you join NSA.

2. Use of the NSA logo and NSA name in your marketing.

3. Listing in their directory and website.

4. Subscription to Speaker magazine, and the opportunity to write for it.

5. Members-only cutting-edge tools and resources.

6. In-person and virtual courses of study in professional speaking.

7. Inclusion in the NSA member directory, for professional networking and advice.

8. Reduced registration fees for chapter, regional and national meetings and workshops.

9. Subscription to the Voices of Experience® audio series of content.

10. The ability to be active in chapter leadership.

11. Recognition within the NSA chapter.

12. A sense of community with one's peers.

13. Presence on chapter and national NSA websites.

14. Easier marketing to local meeting planners.

15. Potential chapter or national board membership.

16. The ability to obtain a CSP or CPAE designation.

17. The perception that when you are a full NSA member, you are a "serious player" in the speaking world, as perceived by speaker bureau partners and meeting planners.

18. Increased understanding of the industry and therefore, increased income.

www.nsaspeaker.org/benefits

Why Should You Join The National Speakers Association?

58 Professional Speakers, Trainers, Facilitators, Writers And Coaches Tell Why They Joined NSA.

1. I learned how to be dynamic and entertaining on stage from the best platform professionals in the business.

2. In NSA I was exposed to business opportunities I never dreamed of before that completely changed the way I do business.

3. As a single practitioner, it was a lonely journey. Then I found the wonderful sense of community that NSA engenders.

4. I reap the amazing benefits of the NSA branding program that national has implemented. It sets me apart from non-NSA speakers.

5. I met a number of similar professionals with whom I have made strategic alliances. With one, I even formed an entire new business. I never could have done that without NSA.

6. I appreciate the ethical and professional standards NSA requires of its members. Potential clients can relax when they learn this. They know I am in the industry-leading professional organization.

7. I was able to join a number of special interest groups that allowed me an incredible amount of

face time with the top experts in my fields in the nation, if not the world. Worth the price of membership alone.

8. I constantly get up close and personal (on an informal as well as formal basis) with the real players in this business. It has demystified much of this game for me, and given me confidence.

9. I can pick the phone up anytime I have a problem or need input, from either local, regional or national NSA folks. I call people in NSA I don't even know and they are glad to help me.

10. I have made lasting friends in this great organization.

11. I gained huge confidence and momentum in my business when I aligned myself with the real players in this business. Being around the big-dog go-getters is infectiously motivating.

12. I felt I had arrived home when I joined NSA and discovered how many other professionals had the same business issues as I did, and how open they were to helping others to surmount them. NSA is so friendly!

13. I found other professional organizations so distant and hard to get involved in. NSA had so many opportunities for me to dig in and help, and in turn, learn the business and rub elbows with the pros already making it.

14. The networking opportunities in NSA are fabulous. I know other professionals all around the world now who I can tap for advice, support and new ideas, just by picking up the phone or whipping out an email. The NSA directory makes it easy to connect with others, by topic, location and experience level. It's a highly valuable tool.

15. The meeting and convention "time in the hallways" is gold. I can't tell you how much inside info I have picked up there, stuff you just can't find in any books or articles. NSA-ers are incredibly open to sharing what they know.

16. Once, I had a really tough training design issue that was killing me. In one NSA meeting, I spoke with 5 members who either gave me solutions, or who pointed me in the right direction. I can't believe the resources in this association!

17. I always wondered what the big dogs in this business were like. Last convention I had lunch with 2 famous names and spoke in the hallway with 3 best-selling authors, all of whom were on Oprah and Montel. You can't buy that kind of contact with those people. At NSA, it's a regular thing.

18. I really have benefited from the listing in the NSA Directory and website, both at the regional and national levels. I have actually had a number of inquiries about my services from them.

19. I really look forward to getting my monthly Speaker magazine. The thing is full of tips, insights and inspirational stories that rev me up for another 30 days!

20. The monthly audiotapes or CD's I get from national are a treasure-trove of information about every possible aspect of this business. I turn my car into a university on wheels every day!

21. With my NSA membership, I am eligible to attend the NSA labs at the International Center for Professional Speaking in Arizona. I just saw the top people in the country speak on my exact subject area for 3 days. I was in heaven!

22. With my NSA membership, I am eligible to sit in on expert coaching sessions at meetings and conventions, in my specialties. This has been a

huge membership benefit for me. I am sitting in meetings with the people I used to see on TV!

23. With my topic area, I thought I would never be the political type, but I was encouraged to run for the board of directors, and now I have board experience on my resume. I am still amazed that I am on the same board with these big movers and shakers.

24. I have use of the NSA Logo and NSA name on all my marketing materials. That alone adds a lot real professional quality to my stuff and sets me apart from the rest of the field.

25. I never really expected it when I joined, but through helping other NSA-ers I have had them send me referrals as a thank you.

26. I know NSA is not a speaking bureau, nor does it focus on getting its members work in a direct sense, but with all the exposure I get through NSA, I have had quite a few inquiries, with some turning into jobs, all from my presence in NSA marketing materials.

27. I have benefited tremendously from being able to run my articles, manuscripts and other work past colleagues in NSA. They have saved me time, money and, in some cases, embarrassment, from alerting me to potential trouble areas in my work products.

28. Through NSA I found a co-author for the book I have been envisioning for many years.

29. I was able to secure some high-powered testimonials from prominent folks in NSA for my upcoming books and audiotape series.

30. The roundtable format of the Meet The Pros is just so powerful, it's like having my own personal consultant on retainer!

31. Being a member of NSA has increased my understanding of the speaking industry and therefore, increased my income as well.

32. I really appreciate the opportunity to learn through the systematic, strategic competencies NSA has set up for those of us who want to really learn it all.

33. I am excited about the chances to obtain a CPAE or CSP designation.

34. I joined in part to receive reduced fees for the national meetings and workshops.

35. There is the perception that when one is a full member, one is a "serious player" in the speaking world by bureau partners and meeting planners. I wanted that recognition.

36. I wanted the opportunity to become active in chapter leadership, and to gain leadership and organizational skills that can help me in my career.

37. I have experienced a tremendous sense of community with my peers in NSA. NSA is like a family.

38. I see my presence on the chapter website as a very valuable part of membership.

39. I really appreciate the chapter's informal program of marketing to local meeting planners. That gives me more bang for my marketing buck than I can get on my own.

40. Being around high achievers in the speaking business challenges me to continually raise the bar on my levels of personal excellence.

41. Being able to present to my peers in chapter meeting formats was very exciting. It was a chance to test myself, get feedback and serve the membership.

42. My being able to write an article for the chapter newsletter was great exposure. Little did I know that would lead to an invitation to be published in the national magazine. NSA has tons of those little, hidden opportunities.

43. I spoke at a local chapter meeting and did not know a meeting planner was in the audience. We now are doing some business together.

44. This is the first way, far more than books, other organizations or the web, that has shown me the inside secrets of how to work the business side of speaking.

45. I found a group of great vendors for audio, video, CD and printing at my last convention. They must have saved me hundreds, if not thousands of dollars.

46. NSA will dramatically compress your learning curve in this demanding business.

47. The speakers at NSA have inside secrets about the business and are content-heavy, not fluff, like many other organizations use.

48. I wanted to learn how to operate a speaking business. NSA showed me how.

49. I love reading the monthly newsletter on speaking tips on professional speaking that my chapter publishes, and, I can't wait to get my hands on the magazine that national puts out each month. You just can't get the information they have there anywhere else. Those are huge membership benefits.

50. I love that members have the opportunity to showcase their skills at chapter meetings and at special events.

51. I attended the special session on doing a speakers demo video and came away with a video I use every day.

52. I like the continuous reinforcement of my learning with NSA-a chapter meeting almost every other month, 2-4 national labs a year, an eastern and a western workshop (both national-caliber events), a national convention, and monthly learning tools like the national magazine named Speaker, the Voices of Experience® audiotapes, and the regular chapter newsletter, Professionally Speaking. I can stay on a steady learning curve all year.

53. I really appreciate the 6-12 Professional Development Workshops (PDW's) that are held every year. They are presented by chapter experts and cover virtually every topic in the speaking business.

54. If I go to every chapter meeting throughout the year, I will complete what amounts to a speaker school, covering all of NSA's competencies. I feel that really prepares me for the business.

55. I look forward at every chapter meeting to have the chance to sit down and have lunch with some of NSA's top leaders and experts.

56. I love being an integral part of America's only organization of professional speakers. It sets me apart from others in the marketplace.

57. Our NSA chapter is the recognized voice of the speaking profession in our area. They set the standard for platform and speaking business excellence. I like being part of that.

58. I truly respect NSA's dedicated vision of advancing the art and value of experts who speak professionally. NSA holds a high standard in its operation.

" " Quotes On Speaking

It is a great rush to come up with a joke that gets a
good response from the audience. It's gold!

Kevin Nealon

I listen to the audience and try and bounce
with them. All audiences are different.
But they are all homo sapiens.

Eric Idle

When I perform, it's very personal. I'm sharing things I
like, inviting the audience into my room.

Andy Kaufman

Toastmasters

Toastmasters has very little to do with making toasts at social gatherings. It has nothing to do with making breakfast toast. Toastmasters has everything to do with your future speaking success!

Toastmasters mission statement: "Through its member clubs, Toastmasters International helps men and women learn the arts of speaking, listening, and thinking--vital skills that promote self-actualization, enhance leadership potential, foster human understanding, and contribute to the betterment of mankind."

Toastmasters International (TI) is an organization you may find extremely beneficial to your career. With over 345,000 members and over 15,900 clubs in 142 countries, Toastmasters is the essential training ground for speakers who want to practice, get exposure, get coaching and be surrounded by supportive, fellow speakers.

Toastmasters is a non-profit that helps its members improve leadership, communication and presentation skills. Virtually every town has at least one Toastmasters club. Indeed, many larger towns, and all cities have dozens. Some Toastmasters clubs specialize, and others are general in nature. Some Toastmasters clubs specialize in humor, storytelling, technical or scientific presentations, etc.

Thousands of organizations, including nationally known firms, sponsor in-house Toastmasters clubs for communication training for their employees.

Toastmaster members can work toward specific educational goals, following both a communication track and a leadership track. The ultimate educational award is Distinguished Toastmaster, which recognizes both tracks. Self-paced Toastmasters programs proceed in logical sequences that help members build critical speaking and leadership skills.

Many NSA members started out in Toastmasters, and many NSA members are still associated with Toastmasters in one capacity or another. Both of us have spoken at many Toastmasters clubs, even when while we were professional speakers. It's a great place to try out new material before you "take it on the road".

We strongly suggest you look into Toastmasters.

www.toastmasters.org

❝ ❞ Quotes On Speaking

I don't think anyone ever gets over the surprise
of how differently one audience's reaction
is from another.

Dick Cavett

You've got to keep your finger on the pulse of what your
audience is thinking, and know what they'll accept from
you.

Dwayne Johnson

When you really need help, people will respond.
Sincerity means dropping the image facade and showing
a willingness to be vulnerable. Tell it the way it is, lumps
and all. Don't worry if your presentation isn't perfect;
ask from your heart. Keep it simple, and people will
open up to you.

Jack Canfield

SpeakerNet News

SpeakerNet News is a free weekly email newsletter sent each Friday to nearly 9000 professional speakers, consultants, trainers, and authors. We highly recommend this resource as a "must-read" each week.

www.speakernetnews.com

Every Friday this informative ezine includes items sent in by the newsletter readers themselves, including tips and strategies on these subjects, and more:

1. Technology, travel, sales and marketing, platform skills, product development, high tech in speaking, negotiating, contracts, handling tough audiences, working with meeting planners and bureaus, public relations, and every imaginable aspect of the speaking business.

2. Products and services of interest to speakers.

3. Want ads selling equipment from the speaking industry, and requests seeking the same.

4. Requests from readers for information and advice.

On the SNN website there is an extensive set of hundreds of compilations across an impressive array of seven topic areas:

- Sales & Marketing
- Better Presentations
- Running Your Business
- Creating Books and Products
- Technology
- Media

- Travel

www.speakernetnews.com/post/index.html

They host a series of teleseminars featuring well-known experts and authorities in the speaking industry. These presenters are speakers, meeting planners, bureau owners, media people, writers, and anyone else connected to professional speaking, or who can help professional speakers.

SpeakerNet News is run by Ken Braly and Rebecca Morgan, long-time NSA Northern California Chapter members.

Quotes On Speaking

The most precious things in speech
are the pauses.

Sir Ralph Richardson

There are three things to aim at in public speaking: first,
to get into your subject, then to get your subject into
yourself, and lastly, to get your subject into the heart of
your audience.

Alexander Gregg

The very best impromptu speeches are the ones written
well in advance.

Ruth Gordon

Business
Resources
For Speaking

Pre-Program Questionnaire (PPQ)

Hello _____,

Thanks again for all your help.

I am really looking forward to meeting you and the other attendees at the _____ Program. To help me customize the program I was wondering if you could complete as much of this questionnaire as you think would be relevant. I really appreciate your help!

If it's easier, you may just want to send this back via email with comments in the spaces provided. Alternatively, I would be happy to phone you for a brief chat to fill the form out together.

Thanks again!

Best Regards,

Bill Cole

This pre-program questionnaire is for Bill Cole's presentation to your group on

_____.

We need your help!! We would like to specifically meet your needs with my presentation. Please take a few moments and help us.

We have filled out the answers to the questions below to the best of our knowledge. Please double check our answers and make additions and corrections. Fill in the questions we left blank. We were uncertain of this information and thought it best for you to provide it to us.

Return this questionnaire to:

William B. Cole Consultants
19925 Stevens Creek Blvd.
Suite 100
Cupertino, CA 95014-2358 USA

Or email it to Bill@MentalGameCoach.com

No later than _____

If you have any questions, call 408-725-7291, or fax 408-440-2398.

Presentation title:

Possible Talk Themes:

Conference/meeting theme?

What is the specific purpose of this meeting (awards banquet, annual meeting etc.)?

What is the theme of this specific meeting?

What are you hoping to accomplish with this meeting?

Why do you think I'll be an asset to this meeting?

What are you hoping to accomplish with my particular program?

How will you know if my program is successful? Please give me a target.

Are there any particular topics or ideas that I should address during my program?

Are there any sensitive issues that should be avoided?

Date   Start time

End time   Breaks?

What is on the program just before I speak?

Will I be able to have some staging set-up time right before I speak?

If I go on right after another speaker, or with no staging set-up time due to program restrictions, when can I arrive to set up my staging area?

What happens on the program right after I speak?

When does your meeting begin? (date and time)

When does it end? (date and time)

Audience dress code for the meeting?

Do you want me to write an article for your newsletter or other publications prior to my program?

What is your desired program mix?

% Motivation

% How To/Nuts & Bolts

What is the audience's overall opinion regarding the subject of my presentation? (favorable, hostile, neutral?)

Please list some industry-specific terms, phrases, jargon or acronyms that I might incorporate into my program.

Please list any humorous buzz-words, pet peeves or inside jokes in your industry or organization I might use for humorous material.

Please share any "local color" (humorous goings-on) you may be aware of relating to the location where my program will be held.

Introducer's name and title?

Work Phone

Meeting-site phone

E-mail

Would someone be able to assist me just before my program ends in collecting program evaluations in return for a raffling of a valuable prize?

Is there any publicity work I can do for you while I am at your event? Radio or television? Please let us know ahead of time, so we can arrange travel.

Who are the other speakers on the program?

Speaker

Topic

Speaker

Topic

Speaker

Topic

What speakers have you used in the past that covered topics related to the material I will be presenting to you?

What professional speakers have you used in the past and what did they speak on?

What did you like and/or dislike? Without their names if you would like, but please comment on the material they used.

Name three main movers and shakers of your group that will be in my audience. With your permission we would like to contact them for more information on your group.

Name

Phone

Name

Phone

Name

Phone

What would make my presentation really "special" for your group?

The Audience Demographics

Number attending?

% Female?

% Male?

% of Guests?

Spouses attending?

Average age of attendees?

Annual average income?

Income range?

Educational background?

Major job responsibilities of audience?

% Senior executives:

% Board of directors

% Admin./clerical

% Mid-management

% Officers/sales reps

% Entrepreneurs

Ethnic diversity?

% Caucasian

% Hispanic

% Black

% Asian

% Other

Positions/Job Titles?

Details About Your Audience

Is their attendance at your meeting mandatory?

At my program?

Will attendees be charged a fee for attending?

If so, what amount?

Please describe what the audience will be doing in the hour preceding my program.

What will they be doing after my program?

What should I know about the people in your group before I start my program? Are their any problems, competition, resentment or peer pressure that I should be aware of?

Their challenges?

Their breakthroughs?

What are the most significant things on their minds as they come to this meeting?

Are there any hearing or sight-impaired individuals who will attend my program?

What separates your high performance people from others?

Tell Us About Your Industry

Problems?

Challenges?

Breakthroughs?

Tell Us About Your Organization

Problems?

Challenges?

Breakthroughs?

What are the greatest accomplishments of this group?

What are the current projects of this group?

Significant events? Mergers? Relocations?

Will my presentation be audiotaped and/or videotaped?

If you wish, I will make my educational materials available to your audience, so that they may continue the learning process at home. There are two ways this can be arranged. Please check the one that is most appropriate for your group.

A. _____ Group purchase in advance for each attendee, at wholesale.

☐ Deliver before the program

☐ Deliver at the end of the program

B. _____ Materials made available at the back of the room after the presentation.

If you checked "B", please make sure that:

Nothing will be on the program directly after my presentation and that there will be a break for at least 20 minutes.

A table will be made available for me to place my materials by the exit door.

Someone from your group will assist with sales.

Travel Information

Location of presentation and venue name

What time can we get into the room to set up?

Who would the contact person be to allow us entry?

Address

Phone

Location at the site itself?

Airport to arrive at

How will I be transported from the airport to your site?

Taxi?

Rental car?

Pick-up person?

My own vehicle?

Pick-up person's name?

Phone

If an emergency occurs on the way to the site, who would be an alternate contact if you are unavailable?

Name and title

Business phone

Home phone

On-site phone

Pager

What is your organization's WEBSITE address?

We can provide free articles for your website, ezine or hard-copy newsletter. What topics would you like? (For an overview, see our website).

What deadlines do you have for inclusion of these articles?

On the website?

For your e-zine?

For your hard-copy publications?

What is YOUR e-mail address?

Thank you very much for your help in making our presentation a success!! We are looking forward to working with you closely to make sure everyone has a good time and leaves the program with valuable information.

Bill Cole, MS MA

PS--Please send us any printed information on your group that may help us such as:

1. Corporate reports

2. Association magazine/newsletter

3. Key product brochures

4. News releases on this presentation

5. Informative articles

6. Past convention programs

7. This presentation's program/brochure

8. Service recognition programs

9. Organization chart

10. Service standards

11. Staff/company newsletter

12. Mission/vision/values

13. Training programs-table of contents

14. Sample sales tracking reports

15. Special promotions/campaigns

16. Meeting agenda/invitation

17. Service measurement tools

18. Sample completed performance appraisal

19. Strategic plan/objectives

20. Business/marketing plan

21. Job descriptions

22. Customer/member newsletter

❝ ❞ Quotes On Speaking

The only thing I miss from the sitcom format is that
immediate gratification of when you're,
if we're talking about comedy,
with the live audience.

Ray Romano

I love working with an audience. I love working with
actual people who, you know, if they're moved, you see
it. If you say something they're stunned by, you see
their jaws drop.
If they're amused, they laugh - that kind of
reinforcement, I totally adore.

Jane Pauley

You're out there on a high wire without a net, and that's
the way actors operate. They have to be fearless about
how they work and they have to create a life for the
audience in 90 minutes
and make them believe.

Charles Durning

Pre-Program Welcome And Questionnaire To Attendees

Dear Attendee,

I am looking forward to your participation in my April 15th presentation, The Mental Game Of Speaking: Peak Performance For Presenters. This program will focus on how to achieve peak performance. We will not directly address platform mechanics, staging, topic development or speech construction. What we will learn, however, is how to be more polished, more at ease and more connected to our audience and to bring forth our best performances more often, when we need them most.

Here are some questions for you to review and bring with you (in your head or on paper) to the presentation. Your answers can remain private if you wish, but please read these questions now, so the presentation has more meaning for you If you wish, you may send these to me in advance.

1. How do you define peak performance on the platform?

2. How would you rate yourself in your ability to handle speaker's nerves?

3. What approaches have you used in your attempts to handle speaker's nerves?

4. Which ones have worked?

5. Which ones have not worked?

6. What system do you use now to achieve inspired, top-level performance when you speak?

7. Describe your best performance when speaking. What was that experience like?

8. Describe your worst performance when speaking. What was that experience like?

Please answer the following questions and return to Bill Cole by fax, e-mail or snail mail prior to the program.

1. What about the art of performing do you hope to learn?

2. What performance tools and skills do you want to leave with?

3. What is your background in attending presentation skills trainings?

4. What is your experience level as a speaker? (Starting, 5 years, 10 years, veteran, etc.)

5. What is your background in any type of peak performance, sport psychology, stress management or self-improvement training?

Wear comfortable clothing on April 15th. We will be active with indoor games and group experiences. The room is large, so bring extra layers just in case. Food and drink will be provided, so if you will be unable to attend, please let us know as far in advance as possible to make the head count accurate and to help reduce costs.

There will be plenty of break time for networking so bring your elevator speech and lots of business cards! Also, bring at least one humorous platform performance experience to share that either happened to you, or that you observed as an audience member.

Please let me know how I can make your participation more valuable and rewarding. I am looking forward to seeing you!!

Best Regards,

Bill

Bill Cole, MS, MA
William B. Cole Consultants
19925 Stevens Creek Blvd.
Suite 100
Cupertino, CA 95014-2358 USA
VOICE: 408-725-7191
TOLL FREE: 888-445-0291
FAX: 408-440-2398
Bill@MentalGameCoach.com
www.MentalGameCoach.com

❝ ❞
Quotes On Speaking

I don't know, on a sitcom, and in theatre especially, you have to really be listening to an audience. And if you're losing them, you can hear the sniffs, and the playbills shuffling and whatnot.

Neil Patrick Harris

I think it's important for me, for my crew and for the audience to bring something new to each show. I have friends who have done the same act, word for word for word, for 20 years. I have a problem with that. I think the audience should see something new in each show.

Carrot Top

Laughter is much more important than applause. Applause is almost a duty. Laughter is a reward.

Carol Channing

The Trade Program

Bill Cole, MS, MA

Many speakers use a unique strategy for getting new clients and other benefits called a "trade program". In return for a free brief talk, you will receive numerous benefits, and you'll hope to sell the firm on your services, in addition to providing them with an immediately useful and entertaining program. This is a showcase, and a barter arrangement in essence.

As an emerging professional speaker, this may be one of your best avenues for getting work. Even though you don't get paid money for doing this, at the very least, you can receive goods, services and benefits that add to up to significant value, almost as good as cash:

1. Testimonials

2. Practice

3. A venue to test new material with a live audience

4. Their name for your client list

5. Insights about yourself as a speaker

6. A chance to sell yourself in front of decision-makers

7. Leads for more clients

8. Possible coaching clients

9. Product sales

10. Mailing list of attendees to whom you can market

11. Talk evaluation by all attendees (This is the sheet where the audience will give you testimonials).

12. Audio and/or videotape of your session

13. Space to put your articles in their publications

Here's the letter. You can have your friend or contact, who is in this target business, contact their boss and then you will set up the free talk and go from there.

Be sure to put in writing whatever trade or barter items you want in return for the talk. Here is a sample letter.

Date

Mr. Steve Somebody
Some Name Business
554 Name Avenue
Silicon Valley, CA 95128

Dear Steve,

It was a pleasure speaking with you on the telephone recently about your business. This letter will confirm that I will be speaking to your group on Thursday, October 21, at your luncheon for approximately 45 minutes in San Jose.

I am a coach who helps individuals and organizations raise the bar on peak performance in their professional and personal lives. I offer a limited number of complimentary presentations on peak performance to organizations every year and am happy to extend this offer to your group.

I am offering this presentation to selected businesses to assist me in gathering new material for my next book, in progress, The Mental Game Of Selling. This presentation will add immediate value to your people's productivity. If my presentation makes sense for your people, and I can offer your organization genuine value, we can discuss furthering our relationship at a later time.

In return for my doing a needs assessment for your group, delivering a customized 45 minute presentation, program handouts, conducting an email follow-up with attendees, and providing you with an article for your newsletter or ezine, I would receive the following:

- A five-minute one-page written evaluation by each audience member on my one-page form that I supply.

- A letter of thanks from your organization on your letterhead.

217

- Granting the use of your company name on my client list.

- A group photograph with the attendees.

- Names of organizations and contact people you would recommend I contact for additional programs.

- Audio and videotape capabilities to tape my program.

I am really looking forward to meeting everyone and to delivering an exciting, valuable program for your company.

Sincerely,

Bill Cole, MS, MA
President
Attached:
Pre-program questionnaire
Room set-up form
Press kit
Photo for your newsletter and website
Article for your newsletter and website

Quotes On Speaking

Well, I'm not one of those people who needs the limelight. If I'm performing, that's what I'm doing. If I'm not, I don't long for it. I don't need the approval of an audience, or applause.

Patti Smith

From day one, I got addicted to being on stage and getting the applause and laughter.

Zac Efron

I still get a little nervous before performing. You don't want to forget a lyric; you don't want to make a mistake. I still get butterflies. You can try to judge an audience, but you can only really judge things by the applause.

Tony Bennett

Speaking Program Action Checklist

Bill Cole, MS, MA

Client _____

Program Title _____

Location _____

Date _____

Time and Length _____

Contact Person and Title _____

Business Phone _____

Cell Phone _____

E-Mail _____

Billing Address _____

Website _____

Pre-Program

Date Completion   Date Completed

Required   or Confirmed

CONTRACTS AND FINANCES

- ☐ Speaking fees one sheet sent
- ☐ Speaking trade-outs one sheet sent
- ☐ Agreement sent
- ☐ Agreement received
- ☐ Agreement signed by both parties and returned to each
- ☐ Invoice for deposit sent
- ☐ Deposit of $_____ received, on date: _____
- ☐ Taxi/shuttle to airport-San Jose
- ☐ Taxi/shuttle from airport-San Jose
- ☐ Taxi/shuttle to airport-at hotel
- ☐ Taxi/shuttle from airport-at hotel
- ☐ Plane tickets-you make and get reimbursed
- ☐ Plane tickets-host makes and gets reimbursed
- ☐ Other transportation
- ☐ Car rental
- ☐ Parking fees
- ☐ Hotel billed directly to host
- ☐ Hotel will be reimbursed to you
- ☐ Hotel reservations confirmed
- ☐ Food, per diem, no receipts.

- ☐ Copies for handouts if you print
- ☐ Postage/mailing for handouts if you mail
- ☐ Expenses NOT to invoice: list- Tips for travel, in hotel
- ☐ Expense receipts gathered/credit card statements
- ☐ Invoice for expenses sent
- ☐ Check for expenses received
- ☐ Check available in person after program

Promotions

- ☐ Promotional materials sent/directed to website

    ☐ Photo   ☐ Bio

    ☐ Articles   ☐ Testimonials

Travel

- ☐ Taxi reservation made
- ☐ Plane reservations made
- ☐ Airport parking reservation made
- ☐ Hotel confirmation received
- ☐ Hotel shuttle confirmation received

Handouts To Helpers

- ☐ PPQ sent
- ☐ PPQ returned
- ☐ Contact with introducer made

☐   Introduction sent to introducer

☐   Room set-up sent

Handouts

Attendee's materials sent to:

        ☐ Hotel   ☐ Client

        ☐ Other _____

☐   Attendee's materials duplicated by client

☐   Your extra handouts carried by you

Your Products

☐   Your books

☐   Your CD's

Your Equipment

☐   Your equipment

☐   Your Olympus digital recorder

☐   Props, posters and magic items

Your Notes

☐   Your notes you take on stage

☐   Your extra handouts

☐   Your extra handouts

☐   Your extra handouts

Post Program

☐   Testimonial letter request sent to client

☐ Testimonial letter received

☐ Letter for request for referrals sent to client

☐ Letter for request for referrals returned

☐ Letter/gift of your thank you sent to client

☐ Letter/gift of your thank you sent to introducer

☐ Letter of your thank you sent to helpers

☐ Read and code evaluations for info requests

☐ Calls to attendees requesting info

☐ Mail outs to attendees requesting info

☐ Extraction of best testimonials

☐ Best testimonials into one sheet, etc.

☐ BC notes re performance improvement

☐ BC reviews audio and video tape

☐ Attendees names onto mailing list

☐ Follow-up program with attendees

☐ Time-limited sale offer to attendees mailed

☐ File 2 sets of attendee handouts

☐ Toss rest of attendee handouts

☐ File unused speaker rating forms, bios, articles

☐ Re-pack all items and ready them for next program

❝ ❞ Quotes On Speaking

I need the applause.

Jerry Lewis

My mother used to tell this corny story about how the doctor smacked me on the behind when I was born and I thought it was applause, and I have been looking for it ever since.

Kathy Bates

If I could sew comedy and philosophy together, then I've done a good job. The primary goal is always going to be laughs and the secondary goal is always going to be saying something without it being a lecture.

Hal Sparks

Presentation Analysis Chart

Bill Cole, MS, MA.

Name _____

Date and Time of Speech _____

Type of Speech _____

Location of Speech _____

Rate your performance in this presentation from 1-5, with 5 excellent, 4 very good, 3 average, 2 fair and 1 poor. This presentation: _____. Now write your answers to these questions.

1. What did you really LIKE about your performance in this presentation?

2. What do you wish you WOULD have done this time?

3. What do you wish you HAD NOT done this time?

4. How was YOUR INTRODUCTION by another person?

5. How was your START to your presentation?

6. How was your CLOSE to your presentation?

7. How was the QUESTION-ANSWER period in your presentation?

8. What was your GAME PLAN (What were you attempting to accomplish, and how?) going into this presentation?

9. What strategies did you ACTUALLY USE in this presentation?

10. What strategies worked WELL?

11. What strategies did NOT work well?

12. How was your audience CONNECTION AND RAPPORT?

13. Were there any heckler or audience DISRUPTION/ RESISTANCE SITUATIONS and if so, how did you handle them?

14. What FEEDBACK (direct and indirect, verbal and non-verbal) did people give you?

15. What IMPACT do you believe your presentation had on the audience?

16. What would you do DIFFERENTLY next time?

17. Overall, how was your MENTAL GAME (nerves, getting into the zone, etc)?

18. How well did the TECHNICAL ASPECTS (lighting, sound, visual) of your program work out?

19. How well did the AUDIENCE HANDOUTS (workbook, manual, etc.) in your program work out?

20. How well did you control the overall ROOM DYNAMICS (staging, assistants, room configuration, etc), before, during and after the program?

21. In a nutshell, why did you SUCCEED, or why did you NOT SUCCEED?

22. If you had this presentation TO DO OVER AGAIN, what would you do DIFFERENTLY?

23. What did you LEARN from this presentation?

24. What will you do DIFFERENTLY IN YOUR PRACTICES and training to benefit from the wisdom you gained from this presentation?

Quotes On Speaking

They may forget what you said, but they will never forget how you made them feel.

Carl W. Buechner

There are only two types of speakers in the world. 1. The nervous and 2. Liars.

Mark Twain

Giving back, doing motivational speeches and stuff like that, that's always made me feel good. If you repeatedly go out there,
and you are the change that you want to see, then that's what you are.

Keke Palmer

Speaking Program Equipment Checklist Request

To make Bill Cole's program as successful as possible, the following equipment will be needed. If there is any question or difficulty in securing the equipment, please call and discuss it with us well before the program. Excellent programs are based on taking care of all the little details ahead of time. We do everything we can from our end to do make everything run smoothly. We appreciate everything you can do from your end!

Audio Equipment Needed:

_____ lavalier microphone

_____ 25 foot Microphone cord

_____ cordless lavalier microphone

_____ we will supply our own cordless microphone

Visual Equipment Needed:

_____ slide projector with remote slide changer

_____ VCR and large screen monitor

_____ large projector screen

_____ overhead projector

_____ free-standing easel with paper pad attached

Dr. Michael Soon Lee, CSP – Bill Cole, MS, MA

Other Equipment Needed:

_____ stool

_____ music stand

_____ lectern

_____ 6 foot draped table at front of room

_____ 6 foot draped table at front of room

Quotes On Speaking

Public speaking is the art of diluting a two-minute idea
with a two-hour vocabulary.

John Fitzgerald Kennedy

There are certain things in which mediocrity is not to be
endured, such as poetry, music,
painting, public speaking.

Jean de la Bruyere

I don't write the books. God writes the books
and delivers the speeches.

Wayne Dyer

Speaking Program
One Sheet Examples

One Sheet For Bill Cole, MS, MA

Are You Reaching Your Platform Potential?
Improve Your Speaking Effectiveness In This Unique Program-

The Mental Game Of Speaking™
Building Composure, Confidence and Credibility

Platform professionals consistently perform to their true potential. They connect with their audiences. They overcome stage fright, get into the zone and influence people in masterful ways. They know how to meet the needs of every audience they encounter. You can do all this and more when you learn the mastery secrets of professional speakers. This program will positively impact your platform confidence and speaking effectiveness.

The Mental Game Of Speaking™ helps you dramatically increase your awareness as a speaker, develop a self-coaching system and gives you a master performance blueprint for realizing your great platform potential. This is a content-rich, practical and experiential program where you will learn how to craft magical stories, use humor, inject a spirit of Hollywood into your staging and come across as the strong professional you are.

Bill was a member of the Board Of Directors of The National Speakers Association in Northern California for two years. He has trained professional speakers and corporate executives in the methods and approaches that world-class presenters utilize. He will teach you how to build a tool kit of communication and influencing skills that you will begin using immediately and will have for a lifetime. Here are some of the powerful benefits you'll receive from this experiential, entertaining and practical program. You will:

239

- **Know how to construct a head message and heart message your audiences will love.**
- **Learn to read your audience so you can think on your feet and adjust your material to their needs.**
- **Discover how to handle disruptions and distractions and stay focused.**
- **Develop interactive audience-involvement approaches to keep everyone engaged.**
- **Look forward to holding Q and A sessions and being spontaneous.**

In this program you will learn inside professional secrets of how to calibrate your audience, use facilitation techniques, pre-program questionnaires, and to craft powerful openers and closers that will make your presentations memorable. You'll learn how to create, write and stage your speeches. You'll learn how to project your body language, voice control and how to pace your speeches.

Available as a breakfast, luncheon or dinner keynote speech, or as a half-day or full day interactive workshop, **The Mental Game Of Speaking™** can be fully customized for your group's needs. Organizations can use this program in retreats, meetings, team sessions and more.

Your platform coach is Bill Cole, MS, MA, The Mental Game Coach™ - Bill is a nationally and internationally-recognized coach and expert in peak performance. He has been a professional coach for over 30 years, including corporate America, big-time college athletics and major-league pro sports. He's a published book author with over 300 published articles worldwide to his credit.

Ask about these other winning programs: **The Mental Game of Customer Service, Winning the Mental Game of Team Building, Winning the Mental Game of Golf, Winning the Mental Game of Life, The**

Mental Game of Selling, Influencing Skills For Leaders, Stop Stress And Banish Burnout For Sustainable Self-Renewal and Coaching For Communication Excellence.

To book this program, or for more information, please contact us today.

WILLIAM B. COLE CONSULTANTS - Peak Performance Solutions Coaching, Consulting, Facilitating, Workshops, Seminars, Speaking, Development, Learning Tools 19925 Stevens Creek Blvd., Suite 100, Cupertino, CA 95014-2358 Voice: 408-725-7191 TOLL FREE: 888-445-0291 Fax: 408-298-9525 E-mail: Bill@MentalGameCoach.com Web Site: www.MentalGameCoach.com

From this source:

www.mentalgamecoach.com/Programs/MentalGameOfS peaking.html

" " Quotes On Speaking

The very best impromptu speeches are the ones written well in advance.

Ruth Gordon

Unaccustomed as most individuals are to public speaking they still do it.

Anonymous

What this country needs is less public speaking and more private thinking.

Roscoe Drummond

One Sheet For
Dr. Michael Lee, CSP

Selling to Multicultural Customers

Dr. Michael Soon Lee

Once you have attracted new customers to your business through a planned multicultural marketing campaign then what do you do with them? Hispanics, African Americans, Asians and Middle Easterners do not buy products and services in the same way as Caucasian customers. If you do not customize your products, services, sales presentation and more to meet the unique need of the fastest-growing consumer group in America, you are wasting your marketing dollars!

Some of the benefits you will receive from attending this program include:

- How people around the word differ in buying habits.

- How negotiation styles impact the purchase process.

- Properly meeting and greeting people from other cultures.

- Overcoming language barriers in selling.

- Learning what products minorities want.

- Learning what services minorities want.

- Building rapport with people from different cultures.

- What people want in a retailer.

- Overcoming price objections.

- Making your store attractive to specific groups.

- Attracting and keeping minority employees.

Target Audience

- Specially designed for companies that sell to multicultural customers.

- Program Format

- From a 60-minute keynote to 3-day workshop to consulting.

- Customized to meet the unique needs of your company and its customers.

About the Presenter

Michael Soon Lee, MBA, is both a multicultural and marketing expert. He has written numerous books and articles on the subject over the past ten years. Mr. Lee has been a marketing director for the State of California and a producer for the ABC Television Network. He presents marketing programs at national conventions and on satellite television. Michael's multicultural programs are well-known throughout the country for being fact-filled as well as fun.

From this source: www.ethnoconnect.com/selling-to-multicultural-customers

Quotes On Speaking

My method is to take the utmost trouble
to find the right thing to say, and then
to say it with the utmost levity.

George Bernard Shaw

I served with General Washington in the Legislature of
Virginia...and...with Doctor Franklin in Congress. I never
heard neither of them
speak ten minutes at a time,
nor to any but the main point.

Thomas Jefferson

Beware of the conversationalist who adds
"In other words".

Robert Morley

Speaking Contract Example

We include here a sample of a speaking contract for professional speaking. Please use this only as a discussion starter with your attorney as you create your own contract. Do not copy this word for word. A contract for a professional speaker will vary from this sample based on the state in which you reside, the nature of your business and other key factors.

The authors and publisher are not engaged in rendering legal advice or services. If assistance of this type is sought, the services of the appropriate, licensed, competent legal professional should be consulted.

LETTER OF AGREEMENT

ABC Company And
Bill Cole, MS MA

ABC Company (hereafter referred to as ABC) agrees to sponsor two conference speaking programs. The first, with a title of "Winning The Mental Game of Life" will be personally presented by Bill Cole, MS MA, on October 18, from 5-5:20pm in Toronto, Canada, for the ABC dealer meeting conference. The type of program will be a keynote speech. Audience size will be approximately 130 people.

The second program, with a title of "Winning The Mental Game of Selling" will be personally presented by Bill Cole, MS MA, on October 19, 2004 in the morning, in Toronto, Canada, for the ABC dealer meeting conference. The length of the program will be 90 minutes in length and the type of program will be a training breakout. Audience size will be approximately 130 people.

All-Inclusive Fee:

ABC will pay one all-inclusive fee of $0000.00 USD that covers airfare, transfers, food, incidentals and the speaking fee for both programs. This price is a substantial discount from Mr. Cole's regular international fee structure. The entire all-inclusive fee will be due at the time of Mr. Cole's final program.

In addition to the all-inclusive fee, ABC agrees to pay lodging for two nights: one Friday prior to the Saturday program, and also the night of the keynote. Lodging shall be at a level of quality at least equal to conference attendees and shall be made by ABC, and billed to ABC at The ABC business address. Hotel room shall be guaranteed late arrival, and guaranteed late checkout.

Audience Handouts & Promotional Materials:

Bill Cole, MS MA will provide promotional materials, a glossy photo, and program descriptions. A master copy of Mr. Cole's standard audience handout materials will be provided for duplication by ABC. Audience handout materials are provided for participant's use only. Materials are copyrighted, and unless specified in the handout materials or in writing in advance, further reproduction of any portion is prohibited. If ABC desires a workbook or extensive set of handouts (beyond the standard audience handout materials), these may be arranged for additional consideration, in advance.

Bill Cole will distribute his "Speaker Rating Form", a one-page sheet that evaluates his "Winning The Mental Game of Selling" program, and asks how he can further help members of the audience. Completion of this form is optional for audience members, but turning in the form makes them eligible for a prize drawing of two

Free to Fee – Resources

hours of free coaching with Bill. This process takes 3-5 minutes or less.

Guarantee & Cancellation:

Confirmed dates for the programs have been decided and customization for the ABC programs has begun. To ensure the date is held and that Bill Cole, MS MA will be available for your program, a non-refundable deposit normally is required.

Bill Cole, MS MA will personally conduct these programs. If, because of physical incapacity or unforeseen or extenuating circumstances, Bill Cole, MS MA is unable to do so, ABC will have the choice of having another speaker conduct the program, or in having Bill Cole, MS MA speak at a future program, both with no cancellation fee, termed a non-refundable deposit. Bill Cole, MS MA is not liable for any expenses relating to this program in the event he is unable to appear. Bill Cole, MS MA has not missed an engagement in his 20 years in business.

Audio & Video Recording:

Bill Cole, MS MA encourages professional audio and video taping of his copyrighted programs. Fees for videotaping are an additional 50% of the speaking program fee, and fees for audiotaping are an additional 33% the speaking program fee. We ask that a professional audio/video technician do the taping, and that we receive two master recordings within 30 days of the program. The performance and material of Bill Cole, MS MA is proprietary. Therefore, copies may not be sold or given out, unless there is a separate written agreement in advance. If ABC desires a particular distribution, a licensing arrangement can be agreed upon. Bill Cole, MS MA retains the copyright and full rights to use these recordings in the future, in any form, in part or in whole.

Product Sales:

If Bill Cole's products are to be sold, a product table will be provided for tapes, CD's and books, and an assistant will be provided to help in the processing of these transactions. Bill Cole, MS, MA will provide this person with a suitable gift as thanks. A product sales form may be included in the participant's handout packet. If this is of interest, Bill Cole, MS MA will send an addendum to this agreement, as any product arrangements must be made in advance. Bill Cole, MS, MA does not "sell from the platform" during his programs.

No product sales or product forms in this Toronto engagement.

Room Set-Up:

Bill Cole, MS MA will be provided one wireless lapel microphone, and one wireless handheld microphone, freely attached to a tall stand, for audience questions.

Risk:

Bill Cole, MS MA hereby gives and agrees to indemnify, hold harmless and defend ABC for any alleged liability resulting from Bill Cole, MS MA presentation, both verbal and written, including libel, slander, violation of copyright, or misstatement of fact.

Termination:

A) This agreement shall be binding for both Bill Cole, MS MA and ABC, and there shall be no right of termination on the part of Bill Cole, MS MA for the purpose of accepting a different engagement on the same date, and there shall be no right of termination on the part of ABC for booking a different speaker for the same engagement.

B) Written notice of cancellation must be made prior to 30 days of the program to Bill Cole, MS, MA to avoid forfeiting the deposit, since most programs are booked months in advance. If your program is rescheduled and we complete it within 12 months of your cancellation, that deposit will be applied to that date.

C) This agreement embodies and contains the entire agreement and understanding of the parties and shall be binding upon their respective heirs, legal representatives, successors and assigns. This agreement may be amended only by writing, and any changes must be signed by both parties.

D) This agreement is entered into the state of California, USA and shall be construed in accordance with and governed by the laws of the state of California, USA.

E) It is mutually agreed that facsimile and PDF versions of this agreement, including signatures are acceptable documents.

_____

Bill Cole, MS, MA

For William B. Cole Consultants

_____

Date

_____

Julie Somebody
Director of Marketing, for ABC
ABC Company
1200 Woodlawn Road West
Guelph, ON, N1H 7K9 Canada

_____

Date

Please make check payable in US funds to William B. Cole Consultants and return to: 19925 Stevens Creek Blvd., Suite 100, Cupertino, CA 95014-2358. Employer ID#: 000-00-0000.

" " Quotes On Speaking

Never stop listening to your audience.

David Copperfield

I am a real ham. I love an audience. I work better with an audience. I am dead, in fact, without one.

Lucille Ball

I didn't have to win, and winning wasn't important to me. Being world champion wasn't important to me. What was important to me was entertaining the audience, and whether that meant winning, losing, singing, or whatever it was on the live show we were doing every week, which was awesome, I was game for it.

Dwayne Johnson

About
The Authors

Dr. Michael Soon Lee

Dr. Michael Soon Lee is the President and Founder of EthnoConnect® which provides seminars, training, consulting and coaching on how to sell more products and services to the multicultural market in America. www.ethnoconnect.com

Dr. Lee has been recognized as one of the Top5 Diversity Speakers in America by the Speakers Platform speakers bureau. He is the first Asian American in history to earn the Certified Speaking Professional (CSP) designation since the founding of the National Speakers Association in 1973. This certification is achieved by only 12% of the membership of the National Speakers Association and less than 10% of the membership of the International Federation for Professional Speakers.

Michael has been speaking for over 15 years and has spoken for over 1,000 clients. He has been a marketing professional and diversity consultant for over three decades. He helps companies reach and increase sales

255

to Hispanics, African Americans, Asians, Middle Easterners, and others. He has been an award-winning salesperson as well as sales manager of both large franchised companies and small independent firms.

Dr. Lee is also the author of eight books including:

- Cross-Cultural Selling for Dummies (Wiley Publishing, 2009)

- Black Belt Negotiating (Amacom Books, 2007)

- Marketing to Multicultural Credit Union Members (Credit Union Executives, 2004)

- Selling to Multicultural New Home Customers (New Home Specialist, 2000)

- Opening Doors: Selling To Multicultural Real Estate Clients (Oakhill Press, 1999)

In addition, he has been a Marketing Director for the State of California, Producer for the ABC Television network, and a Professor of marketing at universities for over 20 years. He is often called as an Expert Witness in court cases where culture is an issue.

Michael holds MBA and DBA (Doctor of Business Administration) degrees from Golden Gate University.

❝ ❞ Quotes On Speaking

Be sincere; be brief; be seated.

Franklin D. Roosevelt

When a sermon at length comes to an end,
people rise and praise God, and they feel
the same way after many other speeches.

John Andrew Holmes

Nothing is as easy to make as a promise this winter
to do something next summer; this is how
commencement speakers are caught.

Sydney J. Harris

Bill Cole, MS, MA

Bill Cole, MS, MA is a nationally-known presentation skills coaching and training expert. He is a speech writer and presentation coach to professional speakers and trainers, executives, business professionals, educators, politicians and everyday folks who just want to give a good speech and not break out in a sweat. www.mentalgamecoach.com

"Bill Cole is a world-class coach...
A speaker's speaker."

National Speakers Association

"a veteran professional communicator"

Linear Technology Corporation

Bill is also one of the most prominent, prolific and successful performance psychology consultants working today. He has been the mental game coach or sports psychology consultant with athletes or coaches of 19 world and national teams, nine international and Olympic teams, 32 professional sports teams, associations or leagues, and of athletes who have won 36 world and national championships. He has been the mental trainer for thousands of athletes in over 100 sports, at all ages and skill levels.

"Bill Cole is a leading Olympic sports psychologist and a world-renowned peak performance coach."

British Broadcasting Corporation (The BBC)

"Bill Cole is a leading author on sports psychology."

Yahoo! Sports

Bill Cole is also the author of ten publications:

Books:

- The Interview Success Guide

- Test Stress Success Manual

- Championship Tennis

- The Mental Game of Golf

- Mental Game of Sports Mental Training Manual

- The Cole Mental Game of Sports Assessment Tool (CMGSAT)

Audiobooks:

- Winning the Mental Game of Life

- Stop Stress And Banish Burnout For Sustainable Self-Renewal

- The Mental Game of Motorcycle Racing

- The Psychology of Golf

Bill holds a BS in Sport Psychology from SUNY-Buffalo, an MS in Physical Education from CSU-Fullerton and an MA in Counseling Psychology from Santa Clara University.

Quotes On Speaking

A speech is poetry: cadence, rhythm, imagery, sweep!
A speech reminds us that words, like children, have the
power to make dance the dullest beanbag of a heart.

Peggy Noonan

The nature of oratory is such that there has always been
a tendency among politicians and clergymen to
oversimplify complex matters. From a pulpit or a
platform even the most conscientious of speakers finds
it very difficult to tell the whole truth.

Aldous Huxley

His speeches left the impression of an army of pompous
phrases moving over the landscape
in search of an idea.

Anonymous

Wanted:

Your Best Tips To Help Others Succeed
In This Rewarding Business

Want to share your great ideas about transitioning into professional speaking with others? Send us your top speaking tips, techniques, success stories, quotes and how-to-tactics that helped you succeed and you can then make a positive impact on others who have an important message to share with the world.

We love feedback. We would really enjoy hearing how you have put the ideas in our book into action and how they have helped you succeed.

We also want to hear from you about issues and challenges we did not include in this first edition. In what areas do you need more help? What do you need to know further to succeed faster?

Reward:

In addition to the good feeling you get in helping others, we want to give you recognition. If we accept your story or success tip we will publish it in our next book, newsletter or article. You will receive credit for the submission, along with a listing of your contact information.

When you send us your tip, be sure to include your name, organization, title, phone number, street address, website and e-mail address. We prefer to receive your submissions via email for easier handling: www.mentalgamecoach.com

We really want to hear from you!

❝❞ Quotes On Speaking

Persuasive speech, and more persuasive sighs, Silence
that spoke and eloquence of eyes.

Homer

Why doesn't the fellow who says, "I'm no speechmaker,"
let it go at that
instead of giving a demonstration?

Kin Hubbard

There are always three speeches, for every one you
actually gave. The one you practiced, the one you gave,
and the one you wish you gave.

Dale Carnegie

Glossary Of Important Terms In The Speaking Business

This glossary contains 218 words and phrases used in the speaking industry.

Ad Lib: Spontaneous or seemingly spontaneous words spoken during a presentation.

Agent: An individual who contracts to represent a speaker or celebrity for a commission.

Amphitheater-Style Seating: Tiered seating like that found in a movie theater.

ASTD: The Association for Training and Development, a professional association for trainers, management consultants and human resources professionals.

Associations: Professional organizations where people with similar interests join to gain educational, professional, financial and social advantages.

Attendees: Anyone who is present at a meeting, convention, program or session where speeches are made.

Audience: Attendees at a program who hear a speaker. (See attendees)

Audience Participation: Having the audience respond or participate, rather than just listen.

Autograph table: A table in the back of the room where a speaker signs books, autographs and other products following a presentation.

A/V: Abbreviation for audio-visual equipment including any multi-media, sound, projection or equipment used in a presentation.

Back Of Room Sales: Product sales that take place at a presentation, often called BOR.

Banquet Style Seating: Where the audience is seated at round tables, usually eight to ten to a table. Very awkward for the person whose back is to the speaker.

Bid: An offer in fee level or payment negotiation a client makes for speaker services.

Bio: A speaker's biography and background, germane to topic and market niche.

Bio Sheet: A one-page speaker's biography and background, germane to topic and market niche.

Blocking: The positioning of you and your equipment on the stage and in the presentation room in relationship to the audience.

Booking: Making an engagement date to speak on a speaker's calendar.

Break-Out: Splitting a larger audience group into smaller units to conduct separate sessions. Sometimes called break-out session.

Breakout Speaker: A speaker who gives 90-minutes to 3-hours of focused content and usually covers one topic in depth and gives the audience an outline to follow.

Bridges: Transitions or connecting points in a speech, from thought to thought. See transition.

Brochure: A promotional flyer or multi-fold piece that contains a speaker's best marketing approaches, such as testimonials, client lists, speech titles and descriptions, bio and contact information.

Bulk Mail: Mail that goes out en mass to reduce postal rates.

Bureau: An agency or booking business that hires speakers for their clients. They are usually paid a percentage of the speaking fee.

Business Card: A small card a speaker gives out to promote his business.

Business Plan: A strategic and tactical formulation that guides a speaker's business in numerous areas, from financial to marketing to operations.

Cancellation clause: The clause in a speaker's contract that specifies the penalties if a program is canceled.

Cancellations: The act of the client calling off a presentation.

Case Study: A detailed, real-world, or contrived example used to highlight and make clear a speaker's concept.

Cavett Award: The highest award in the National Speakers Association, for the speaker of the year.

CEU's: Continuing Educational Units.

Circle Seating Style: Where the audience is seated in a circle around a speaker or presenter.

Classroom Seating Style: Where the audience is seated in parallel rows behind tables facing the speaker.

Client: The entity that pays the speaker, which may be a corporation, association, educational institution, non-profit, or governmental agency.

Closing: The final section of a speech the speaker uses to make a final point or to bring the audience to action.

Cold Calling: Telephone sales calls made to suspects, or to people who do not know the speaker.

Concurrent Session: A break-out session that runs at the same time as other sessions.

Conference-Style Seating: Where the audience is seated in parallel rows without tables facing the speaker.

Consultant: An expert who analyzes a specific business problem and prescribes a solution. He or she may be involved in the carrying out of the solution and may be paid by the hour, day or week or flat project fee.

Consulting: The work a speaker does that does not include speaking or training, such as writing, coaching, assessment, facilitating and advice.

Content: Material in a presentation that is useful beyond mere entertainment value.

Contract: The legal document between the speaker and the agent, bureau, manager or client, containing what each will do and considerations for each.

Convention: A large gathering of people with similar interests where a speaker would present.

Copyrights: Statements and symbols signifying the legal ownership of articles, books, tapes and other products or business names or processes that a speaker produces.

Cordless Microphone: A microphone that uses a transmitter instead of a cord to send the signal to receiver, then to an amplifier, and then to the sound speakers. May be prone to interference from other devices using the same frequency.

Corporate Training: Training that is done for a corporate client, usually on their premises.

Cover Letter: The letter that goes out with a promotional package or press kit, explaining the reason for the mailing.

CPAE: The Council of Peers Award of Excellence: The Hall of Fame for speakers in the National Speakers Association.

Cruise Ship Speaking: Speaking on board ships, sometimes for pay and sometimes for trade of room and board.

CSP: Certified Speaking Professional, the highest earned designation from the National Speakers Association.

Customization: The degree to which a speaker modifies a speech or product material to fit the needs of the client and audience.

Dais: A raised platform the speaker stands on. Also called a podium, riser or stage.

Delivery: What a speaker does during a performance. This is the speaker's style, flair, drama and persona in action.

Demo: An audiotape or videotape used to promote yourself to meeting planners and other potential clients.

Direct Mail: Mail sent to a particular person, rather than to a business or occupant.

Downstage: The part of the stage closest to the audience.

Dynamic Range: The variances in voice, volume, gestures, tone, etc., a speaker may use in a performance.

Easel: A stand used to support visual aids such as flip charts or graphics.

Elevator Speech: A brief (usually 30 seconds or less) advertisement you provide to someone the first time you meet them, describing your services and business.

Emcee: An informal term for the master of ceremonies, or announcer or introducer at a program. Also known as MC.

Emerging Speaker: A speaker new to the speaking profession.

Endorsement: A quote, phrase or letter of testimonial from someone who has seen you speak, attesting to your abilities.

Engagement: A speaking date you have booked. Also called a gig.

Expenses: Any business-related out of pocket expenses incurred while you travel to or from a speaking date.

Extemporaneous: Any spur of the moment, impromptu or spontaneous presentation.

Facilitation: The process of guiding a group through awareness and educational exercises. Some speaking is involved.

Fee: Payment for speaking, consulting, facilitating or other services.

Fee Levels: The various fee segments in the business, ranging from novice, emerging, journeyman, established to celebrity.

Firm Date: A speaking engagement that is confirmed and guaranteed by the client.

Flipchart: The paper you write on that goes on an easel.

Flyer: A circular or piece of marketing collateral you send out to obtain bookings.

Focus: Specific intent of a talk or speech.

Freebies: Trade or gratis speeches you give in return for some or all of the following exposure: practice, testimonials, referrals, bartered goods or services.

General Assembly: The time, other than meal time, when all attendees of a meeting convene.

General Session: The time when all attendees of a meeting convene to hear a keynote.

Gig: A speaking date or engagement.

Give-Aways: Free items the speaker gives to the audience that helps them continue their learning at home and that promotes the speaker.

Glossy: Biography or one-sheet printing on heavy, shiny paper.

Handout: Any paper, report, handbook, workbook or item the speaker gives the audience.

Handheld Microphone: A microphone you use from your hand.

Hands Free Mike: A microphone you wear that either attaches to your lapel or hangs around your neck. Sometimes called a "lavaliere" or "lapel mic".

Head Table: The table where dignitaries, leaders, directors or important guests sit at a luncheon or dinner program.

Heart Story: A story that touches the heart instead of the head.

Heckler: Someone who attempts to interrupt your presentation, either by talking or by making noise.

Honorarium: Small stipend for speaking or related services.

House Lights: Lighting that shines on the audience rather than the speaker.

Humorist: A speaker who uses funny material to entertain and enhance speech content.

Ice-Breakers: Exercises designed to loosen up an audience, to prepare them to receive a speaker and each other.

IGAB: The International Group of Agents and Bureaus, a professional association for businesses that book speakers.

In-Bound Marketing: Turning telephone inquiries into bookings through effective persuasion and sales techniques.

In-House: A presentation made on the client's site.

Introducer: The person who presents a speaker to the audience via a brief speaker bio and lead-in of the speaker's reasons for being there.

Interactive Training: Hands-on or experiential exercises designed to get the audience involved fully, rather than just in a listening mode.

Introduction: A brief biography and reason the speaker is giving the speech, spoken by an introducer.

Impromptu Speech: An extemporaneous speech, devised on the spot.

Island Seating Style: Where audience members sit in groups or "islands".

Keynote: The main speech given to most, if not all, the attendees in one general session.

Keynote Speaker: A speaker who kicks off a conference, usually with 60-90 minutes of motivational and high-energy speaking, using lots of stories and humor with a minimum of content.

Keynoter: The person giving the keynote.

Kill Fee: Payment made to the speaker should the client cancel the program without sufficient notice.

Lavalier: A microphone, with or without a cord, that is either worn around the neck, or attached to clothing. Considered to be a hands-free microphone.

Lectern: A stand for holding the speaker's notes and other speaking equipment and props.

Letter Of Agreement: A legal document between speaker and client, less formal than a contract.

Licensing: The selling of temporary use permits to an organization for a speaker's materials or products.

Master Of Ceremonies: A person who hosts parties and events in an enjoyable manner by keeping events on time, announcing people and program events and setting the proper tone. See MC.

MC: Master of ceremonies.

Mailing House: A business that handles outgoing and/or incoming mail. This may include product orders and fulfillment, mailing lists, newsletters and other products of the speaker.

Mailing List: A list of names a speaker uses to mail marketing material.

Manager: A person who handles a speaker's business details.

Marketing: Efforts directed to promoting, advertising and making a speaker known to a particular niche.

Media Kit: A speaker's press kit sent to potential clients and the media, to promote the speaking business. It may contain a bio, articles, one-sheets, program descriptions, client lists and testimonials. See press kit.

Meeting Planner: The coordinator or organizer in charge of logistics for the entire meeting or convention.

Mentor: An experienced speaker who coaches a less-experienced speaker.

Menu Of Services: The range of services a speaker offers to clients.

Mic: A written abbreviation for the word microphone, pronounced "mike".

Mike: An abbreviation for the word microphone.

Moderator: The person in a panel, debate, roundtable or meeting who controls and organizes its conduct.

Motivational Speaker: A speaker who attempts to inspire, i.e., make the audience behave differently and be entertaining at the same time.

MPI: Acronym for Meeting Planners International.

Multiday: A program presented over more than one day.

Multimedia: The use of varied media to enhance a presentation. This may include slides, computer-generated images, overheads, music, film, video and more.

NSA: Acronym for National Speakers Association.

Newsletter: A regularly mailed hard-copy or electronic report designed to educate clients and promote a speaker's business.

Off The Shelf: A turnkey, standard or boiler-plate speech or program, one that is not customized to the client's needs.

One Sheet: The piece of marketing collateral that announces a speaker's programs, bio, client list, contact information and other branding or marketing information. May be one-sided or two-sided.

On-Site Training: Training provided at the client's place of business.

Opening: The very start of a speech, as the speaker begins after being introduced.

Open Enrollment Program: A speaking, training or workshop program for which the public may enroll.

Outbound Marketing: Communications sent to potential clients via telephone, direct mail, fax, e-mail or other media intended to induce them to book a speaker.

Outline: The brief sketch or speech overview used by a speaker, and possibly used as handout for the audience.

Overhead Projector: An illumination device that shows transparencies on a screen.

PA System: The public address sound system used in a program.

PR (Public Relations): Promotions, advertising, publicity and other strategies used to make the speaker more visibility in a chosen market.

Panel: A group of speakers or experts who discuss a topic, often with question and answer format from the audience.

Partial Exclusive: An exclusive agreement with a speaker in a restricted market segment, either via area or by market niche.

Per Diem: Payment for daily expenses a speaker incurs, or for consulting services per day.

Platform: A dais, riser, podium or stage that the speaker stands on.

Plenary: The general or main session or gathering at a meeting or convention.

Plug: Making a pitch on the platform for a speaker's book, tapes or other products and services.

Podium: A dais, riser, platform or stage that the speaker stands on.

Positioning: How a speaker and or his products and services are specially differentiated in the marketplace.

Power Pack: A group of products sold as a single unit, as a special or sale price, usually at an engagement.

Power Point: A software program from Microsoft® used for making multi-media presentations.

PPQ (Pre-Program Questionnaire): The multiple page assessment tool sent to the client to determine how the program will be customized.

Premiums: Promotional items given to clients or audience members usually containing a speaker's contact information.

Press Kit: The package of information, usually in a folder, used to promote a speaker. It may contain a bio, articles one-sheets, program descriptions client lists and testimonials. See media kit.

Press Release: A promotional notice sent out announcing a news-worthy accomplishment or item by a speaker.

Presentation Software: A computer application used to create and develop multimedia images and sound supporting a speech.

Pricing: The fee and product and services price points a speaker sets.

Professional Speaker: A speaker who is paid a fee or honorarium for a performance.

Product: The books, reports, audios, videos, CD's, workbooks, diskettes, posters, etc. that a speaker sells to the client or to the audience.

Projector: Equipment for illuminating a picture. May be a slide, overhead, computer or movie projector.

Promotion: Usually a discount for a limited time designed to induce meeting planners to try a speaker.

Promotions: Anything designed to increase awareness on the part of meeting planners about a speaker. Could be advertising, public relations or other materials.

Prompter: An electronic display device that projects the speaker's notes onto a screen so they may be read by the speaker, but by no one else. See teleprompter.

Proposal: A suggested outline of services and products a speaker provides to a client for review, for potential purchase.

Prop: Abbreviation for property, any item used by the speaker to enhance his or her performance, including magic items or conversation pieces.

Proprietary: A speaker's original material, products, names or processes owned by the speaker.

Prospects: Potential customers or clients who might hire a speaker.

Public Address System: The sound system used in a program. Also called a PA system

Publicity: Any marketing or promotional activity a speaker does to advance his or her name recognition and visibility in the marketplace.

Public Domain: Material, music, names, titles or other content that is not owned by any individual or business. Anyone may use them.

Public Seminar: Any program available to the public.

Public Speaker: An individual who speaks in public, paid or not.

Q and A: The period of a presentation when the speaker takes questions from the audience. Called question and answer.

Rapport: The intimate, trusting relationship forged between the speaker and the audience.

Rave: A testimonial quote or letter from a satisfied client or meeting planner. See testimonial.

Referral: The name of another business or organization that the speaker may contact for potential future business.

Rehearsal: Practicing or reviewing the presentation, either actually or mentally.

Retreat: A place and time when a group goes away from their normal work setting to reflect, renew and accomplish certain tasks.

Role Playing: A simulation where people take on personas in a dramatic-like manner to make a point about some aspect of business or life.

Room Set-Up: The manner in which the audience seating is set up for a presentation. See seating arrangements.

Sales Cycle: The period of time and various processes the sales pipeline goes through, from initial contact to close of the sale.

Script: A written procedure for conducting a sales call. Also a speaker's written notes.

Seating Arrangements: The manner in which the audience seating is set up for a presentation. See room set-up.

Self-Publishing: The writing, printing, marketing and distribution of a book, audio, video, CD or other product by the speaker alone. Costs are borne by the speaker.

Selling From The Platform: The art of convincing the audience that they need the products and services the speaker makes available during and after the program.

Seminar: A presentation that may be 30 minutes to multiple days in duration.

Seminar Companies: Companies that hire speakers to travel and conduct public programs on various topics.

Seminar Leader: A speaker who gives 3-hours to 6-hours or even several days of very in-depth coverage on one or several topics. Usually provides the audience with a workbook.

Showcase: A free, or usually free, speech a speaker gives to provide exposure to potential clients.

Simulations: A reality-like game or situation where people take on personas in a dramatic-like manner to make a point about some aspect of business or life.

Signature Story: A speaker's original and easily-recognized personal story.

Site-License Fees: Payment a speaker charges a company to use products in their company only, such as manuals, books, tapes, workbooks and assessments.

Slides: Either an overhead transparency or a 35 mm, small transparency going into a slide projector.

Sound Bites: Short, pithy quotes or phrases used to help a speaker be memorable.

Sound Man: The person handling the AV and usually all other multi-media in a presentation.

Sound System: Music or vocal projection equipment used in a program. Also called a PA System

Speaker Rating Sheet: A one-page form evaluating the speaker, filled out by the audience.

Smile Sheet: Same as speaker rating sheet, but may have less detail.

Speech: The actual program a speaker presents to the audience.

Staff: Anyone who assists the speaker, either in the office or on-site.

Stage: Where the speaker stands to deliver the program.

Stage Left: The side of the stage to the performer's left as he faces the audience.

Stage Right: The side of the stage to the performer's right as he faces the audience.

Stage Directions: Physical location points for the speaker to use once on stage during a performance.

Stage Fright: Anxiety or nervousness around a performance.

Suspects: Potential purchasers of a speaker's services or products, who do not know the speaker yet.

Tailoring Material: Customizing presentation material to the client and audience.

Team Building: Developing new or established teams for better trust, cohesion and functioning.

Teleprompter: An electronic display device that projects the speaker's notes onto a screen so they may be read by the speaker, but by no one else. See prompter.

Tentative Date: A hold on a date by the speaker for a client, even though there is no firm commitment from the buyer.

Testimonial: A congratulatory or praising quote or letter from a satisfied client or meeting planner. See rave.

Theater Seating Style: See amphitheater style seating.

Toastmasters International: A world-wide organization of people who focus on the learning and promotion of the art of speaking.

Trade Out: The bartering of speaking services for goods or services, rather than cash-only payment.

Trainer: A person who presents training or workshops or seminars.

Transparency: A clear plastic sheet viewed by light shining through it. Can be written on or materials may be printed on it.

Transitions: Bridges or connecting points in a speech, from thought to thought. See bridge.

Upstage: Position on the stage farthest from the audience. May also refer to one speaker stealing the audience's attention from another.

Ups-Unique-Selling Proposition: That which makes one program or speaker different from another.

U-Shaped Seating Style: Where the audience is seated in a horseshoe arrangement with the speaker positioned at the opening of the "U".

Venue: The place where a meeting, convention or speech takes place.

Visual Aids: Any physical props or projections a speaker uses to enhance the content for the audience.

Website: A visual, and sometimes audio, package a speaker creates for people to visit on the World Wide Web.

Wings: The sides of the stage, out of sight of the audience.

Workshop: A hands-on experiential program lasting from one hour to multiple days.

Workbook: An educational handout, usually multiple pages, a speaker creates for the audience to enhance their understanding of the speech content, and as added take-away value.

" " Quotes On Speaking

His speeches to an hour-glass
Do some resemblance show
Because the longer time they run
The shallower they grow.

Anonymous

The problem with speeches isn't so much
not knowing when to stop,
as knowing when not to begin.

Frances Rodman

Commencement oratory must eschew anything that
smacks of partisan politics, political preference, sex,
religion or unduly firm opinion. Nonetheless, there must
be a speech: Speeches in our culture are the vacuum
that fills a vacuum.

John Kenneth Galbraith

283

Dr. Michael Soon Lee, CSP – Bill Cole, MS, MA

Index

9781931825153